SECRET CHARLOTTE

A GUIDE TO THE WEIRD, WONDERFUL, AND OBSCURE

Sarah Crosland

Copyright © 2017, Reedy Press, LLC
All rights reserved.
Reedy Press
PO Box 5131
St. Louis, MO 63139
www.reedypress.com

No part of this publication may be reproduced or transmitted in any form or by any means, electronic or mechanical, including photocopy, recording, or any information storage and retrieval system, without permission in writing from the publisher. Permissions may be sought directly from Reedy Press at the above mailing address or via our website at www.reedypress.com.

Library of Congress Control Number: 2016955975

ISBN: 9781681060699

Design by Jill Halpin

Printed in the United States of America
17 18 19 20 21 5 4 3 2 1

CONTENTS

1	Introduction
2	Ambrose the Ghost
4	Miraculous Sighting
6	Spooky Symbols
8	Big Head
10	Culinary Creativity
12	Garage Band
14	Breathing Fire at the Ball Game
16	The Hilton Sisters
18	Need for Speed
20	Go for the Gold
22	Scoop of History
24	Home of the Hornets
26	Mint Condition
28	Breaking the Bank
30	Park of the Past
32	Toast to Treehouses
34	Paranormal Activity
36	Bug on a Building
38	Coming Up Roses
40	Up Is Down
42	Making Magic
44	Here's a Tip
46	The Mill Deal
48	Symbolic Statues
50	Home Sweet Home
52	Under Water
54	DC in NC
56	It's a Sign

58	From Cars to Cold War
60	Road of Sharon
62	Bird Watching
64	Buried Treasure
66	Faith on the Farm
68	Italian Style
70	Tales from the Dunhill
72	Love Locks
74	Flower Power
76	News from the North
78	Spinning Wheel
80	Historic Hotdogs
82	By the Letter
84	Lost Lake
86	Interior Plans
88	Set Up Camp
108	Far Eastern Exposure
110	Local Delicacy
112	Presidential Appeal
114	Flight Show
116	Sign of the Times
118	What a Drag
120	Meck Dec
122	Covert Collection
124	Into the Woods
126	The Biblical Bench
128	Transportation Authority
130	Under the Dome
132	Intriguing Intersection
134	Margaret the Mummy
136	Saved by the Bell

Page	Title
138	Off Track
140	Sartorial Statue
142	Think Pink
144	Worm Worries
146	Light Show
148	California Dreaming
150	There Goes the Neighborhood
152	Peek at the Past
154	Find the Shine
156	'Tis the Season
158	Mystery Building on Brevard
160	Holy Grounds
162	Take It to the Bank
164	Presidential Seal of Disapproval
166	Exotic Experience
168	The Scoop on the Coop
170	Looking Up
172	The Big Head
174	Claim to Fame
176	Heads Up
178	Sit. Stay. Drink.
180	Making Waves
182	Hidden Path
184	On Track
186	On Call
188	All Aboard
190	Elephant on the Loose
192	The Uptown Buzz
194	Fantastical Figurines
196	Final Destination
198	Bombs Away

200	Pie in the Sky
202	Home Sweet Home
204	A Grave Affair
206	Something's Fishy
208	The Big Cheese
210	Index

INTRODUCTION

Before I began researching this book, I thought I knew a lot about Charlotte. It turns out, the Queen City still held—and holds—its fair share of secrets. From the unexpected stories behind everyday places to the area's most unusual destinations, much of my work has been a search for answers. But ultimately, it was about asking the questions most of us never think to ask. Why is a pair of British conjoined twins buried in Charlotte? What's beneath the surface of Lake Norman? Why is there a gold leaf eagle above the door of the Mint Museum? Why is a Volkswagen Beetle permanently parked on the roof of Pinky's restaurant? Why does a sign in Uptown point to Edgar, Wisconsin? Where did livermush come from? What ever happened to Heritage USA theme park?
Enter *Secret Charlotte*, your guide to all the things you never knew you wanted to know about your city.

You'll find quite a mix of topics in these pages. From historical stories—and occasionally rumors—to current destinations, Secret Charlotte looks at the city through the lens of the unusual. And while modern Charlotte has a reputation for being pretty straight-laced, this book is full of quirky, cool, and occasionally even creepy sides of the city. These chapters share a side of Charlotte that's been here all along, just waiting to be discovered.

From hidden history to little-known spots, consider this your ultimate scavenger hunt. Each of the items is attached to a site that you'll want to explore—and where hopefully you'll stumble across even more of Charlotte's uniquely wonderful culture.

1 AMBROSE THE GHOST

Is there a haunted tunnel to the city's oldest cemetery?

In 1876, *The Daily Charlotte Observer* ran a story that read that people had seen a white figure walking in front of Charlotte's First Presbyterian Church at night. The headline was "A 'Ghost' in the Church Yard," and it may have begun the rumors of Ambrose, a friendly ghost who doesn't speak, but does linger around the historic church.

The church's sanctuary, which nowadays sits among skyscrapers in Uptown Charlotte, was built in 1857. It's across the street from Old Settlers' Cemetery, where the first grave is dated 1776. According to local lore, as the Union army drew closer to Charlotte during the Civil War, a sextant at First Presbyterian named Ambrose was instructed to build a tunnel beneath 5th Street, between the church and the cemetery.

Ambrose was told to hide the church's valuables in the tunnel. As the story goes, Ambrose returned to retrieve the treasures after the army left, and the tunnel unexpectedly collapsed, killing him.

While Old Settlers' Cemetery recently underwent a $500,000 restoration, the historic graveyard still shows signs of its age, with many broken headstones. However, its old oak trees and brick paths continue to make it a popular spot for a stroll for uptown dwellers.

OLD SETTLERS' CEMETERY

WHAT A historic graveyard

WHERE Uptown Charlotte at the corner of Fifth and Church Streets

COST Free

PRO TIP On your visit, also look for the gravesites of prominent people buried here, including Thomas Polk, a Charlotte founding father and the great-uncle of President James K. Polk.

Old Settler's cemetery, which is across the street from First Presbyterian Church, covers one block in Uptown Charlotte and is the city's oldest official cemetery, with graves dating from 1776.

    Today, there's no sign of the tunnel and there's no actual record of Ambrose—other than those who say they've heard him in the church's creaking corridors and tinkling chandeliers.

2 MIRACULOUS SIGHTING

Where can you see a plane that crash-landed with more than 150 people inside—and everyone survived?

US Airways Flight 1549 was headed from La Guardia airport to Charlotte on January 15, 2009. So, it makes sense that this Airbus A320's final landing spot should be at the Carolinas Aviation Museum, which is adjacent to the Charlotte airport.

Shortly after takeoff in New York, at an altitude of 2,818 feet, the plane hit a flock of geese, which caused both of its engines to shut down. The now-famed Captain Chesley "*Sully*" Sullenberger made the fast, life-saving decision to glide the aircraft into a water landing on the icy Hudson River.

Today, the story has been made into the blockbuster movie Sully and endures as one of the most impressive crash landings ever made. While the passengers themselves all safely made it off the plane that day, it took several

---

Since the Airbus A-320 crash-landed into New York's Hudson river, it was a long trip to bring it to Charlotte. First, it had to be pulled from the river and onto a barge. Then, its wings were temporarily removed to truck it to North Carolina. And finally, it was reassembled inside the museum.

Carolinas Aviation Museum, which is located on the grounds of Charlotte Douglas International Airport, was the final resting place for US Airways Flight 1549, now known as the Miracle on the Hudson.

months for the plane itself to be removed from the river.

Passengers from the flight—and, of course, Sully—have been allowed on the plane, but visitors to the museum can only view its exterior. However, it's a thorough and impressive exhibit featuring passenger stories and videos.

CAROLINAS AVIATION MUSEUM

WHAT A museum focused on flight

WHERE 4672 1st Flight Dr., near Charlotte Douglas Airport

COST General admission is $12

PRO TIP The museum, which is very large and filled with planes, is not air-conditioned. So, plan your visit for a cooler day.

3 SPOOKY SYMBOLS

Are the murals inside of Uptown's Bank of America's corporate center Masonic symbols or simply abstract art?

Uptown Charlotte's tallest building is the Bank of America tower in the center of town. Its impressive, high-ceilinged lobby features three oversized panel frescos that were created in 1992 by artist Benjamin Long. The murals have been praised for their mix of realism and abstract, and they're said to represent themes of building, creativity, and knowledge.

However, others believe there is a darker side to the murals. Images like a checkered floor, a blond-haired boy, a burning bush, a puppet, and a nun all have prompted talk—mostly on conspiracy theory blogs—of Masonic symbols, the Illuminati, and even the apocalypse.

Regardless of whether or not Long's works are representative of something mysterious, they are undeniably eye-catching and a little eerie.

Much of artist Benjamin Long's other work can be found in churches, abbeys, and religious centers. Another one of the Asheville-based artist's frescoes was inside St. Peter's Catholic Church just up North Tryon Street, but was irreparably damaged during construction in 2002.

Inside the Bank of America corporate center in Uptown you'll find three larger-than-life—and eye-catching—frescos depicting themes like building and creativity.

BANK OF AMERICA CORPORATE CENTER

WHAT The ground floor lobby of the bank's corporate headquarters

WHERE 100 N Tryon St., in the center of Uptown

COST Free

PRO TIP The lobby is open to the public, and there is seating in front of the murals if you'd like to rest for a moment as you soak them in.

4 BIG HEAD

Where can you see fourteen tons of steel made into a giant water fountain shaped as a human head?

Sure, it's tucked into a business park south of town, but that doesn't make this modern piece of art by a European sculptor any less impressive.

Count Riprand Arco, the founder of American Asset Corporation, originally conceived the piece. He wanted a stunning and beautiful focal point for the corporation's two-hundred-acre office park—and he definitely got it.

Created in 2007 by renowned Czech artist David Černý, *Metalmorphosis* is a mirrored water fountain. It features 40 pieces of mirrored steel that all rotate 360 degrees, deconstructing and then reconstructing a face as it moves and "spitting" water into the fountain.

It's a mammoth structure, but possibly its most interesting feature is that it is always available for viewing via its webcam (www.metalmorphosis.tv). So keeping tabs on the giant head can be done any time from anywhere.

During the workday this plaza is busy with the office park's employees and even nearby food trucks during lunch. But on weekends it's so quiet that visitors to the sculpture can hear its hum as it rotates, reconstructing its face.

This stunning mirrored water fountain, rotating head by Czech sculptor David Černý unexpectedly located in the center of an office park in South Charlotte.

WHITEHALL CORPORATE CENTER

WHAT The *Metalmorphosis*, a giant head on the center's grand plaza

WHERE 3700 Arco Corporate Dr., in the Steele Creek area of Charlotte

COST Free

PRO TIP Because it is reflective, the sculpture is the most beautiful on especially clear days or at sunset.

5 CULINARY CREATIVITY

What happens when you mix burgers with sushi?

You could simply order a burger and fries at SouthPark's Cowfish Sushi Burger Bar, or you could opt for a traditional sushi roll (there are more than sixty to choose from). But then you'd be missing half the fun of the popular spot's creative menu.

When Charlotte restaurateur Marcus Hall opened Cowfish in 2010, he wanted to include more playful options. His amusingly named idea, "Burgushi," took off, making the spot a fast favorite in Charlotte—and ultimately expanding to Raleigh, Atlanta, and Orlando.

The adventurous eater will enjoy the menu's Burgushi section, which offers variations that include both burger and sushi components (don't panic, there's no raw beef here). There are sushi rolls that include sautéed chipotle bison, Angus beef, and even seared filet mignon. But where things get especially inventive are on the beef sandwiches made with rice-filled "buns."

Can't bring yourself to mix the two? Order one of the bento boxes, which feature both burgers and sushi—served separately.

COWFISH SUSHI BURGER BAR

WHAT A sushi and burger restaurant adjacent to SouthPark Mall

WHERE 4310 Sharon Rd.

COST Mid-level restaurant, varies depending on order

PRO TIP Don't skip dessert. The Apple Pie "Wontons" are another tasty mix of traditional American fare with Asian influences.

At SouthPark's Cowfish Sushi Burger Bar diners can indulge in burgers and sushi—or burgushi. The unusual mix is available in a sushi style, burger style, or, for the slightly less adventurous, a bento box featuring both.

While Burgushi is the most inventive aspect of this popular restaurant, there are plenty of other fun and quirky parts of Cowfish. Colorful art lines its walls and in its bathrooms, you'll hear audio of a woman saying cliché phrases in English followed by the Japanese translation.

6 GARAGE BAND

What is the riddle that, if deciphered, results in a light and sound show at an Uptown parking garage?

In 1998 artist Christopher Janney created the multimedia *Touch My Building* on the side of Uptown's 7th Street parking deck. More than four hundred panels cover the nine-story façade of the building in a variety of colors. These include thirty-foot-tall "light fins," which, when touched, light up and play a mix of melodies.

The wall, which is just outside of 7th Street Market and faces the 7th Street light rail stop, is a favorite for both children and adults who enjoy watching it light up and hearing it play. But in addition to the random play and the hourly vibrant light and sound performances by the panels, there are more mysterious qualities to its tunes.

Occasionally, with no apparent timing, the building will simply play a piece, prompting some to say that a ghost resides within its walls. There is also a riddle on the side of the building, which can be deciphered to play a pattern, and will ultimately result in the building responding with another light and sound show.

The next time you're waiting for the train at 7th Street station, look for the ten-inch plaque on the side of the building. It contains a poem that includes a riddle. Solve it to hit in just the right sequence to light up the blue, purple, and red strips on the building.

7TH STREET PARKING GARAGE

WHAT The eastern facing façade of the Bank of America 7th Street Parking Deck

WHERE 225 E 6th St., adjacent to the 7th Street Market

COST Free

PRO TIP Visit at night, when the light show is especially impressive.

At the 7th Street Station in Uptown you'll find this large wall, which plays music and lights up when you touch it. Read the sign to learn how to solve its riddle to make it play.

7 BREATHING FIRE AT THE BALL GAME

Why does a giant dragon statue emit smoke in the middle of Uptown?

While professional baseball has been around Charlotte for more than a century, the local team wasn't called the Charlotte Knights until 1988. In 1993, the Knights became a Triple-A team and today their major league affiliation is with the Chicago White Sox. But the Knights have stuck closely to their medieval theme, at one point calling their stadium "The Castle" and having a friendly dragon mascot.

In 2014, the team's $54 million BB&T Ballpark opened just in time for the season in the middle of Uptown Charlotte and in 2015 the team unveiled an eighteen-foot dragon statue across the stadium from home plate, deemed Home Run Dragon. Each time that the Knights score a home run—or win the game—the dragon breathes smoke as the crowd cheers.

From beer festivals to private events, BB&T Ballpark is used year-round for much more than baseball. But to see its eighteen-foot Home Run Dragon breathe smoke, you'll have to be there for an actual home run.

BB&T BALLPARK

WHAT Charlotte's Uptown ballpark, home to the Charlotte Knights

WHERE 324 S Mint St., across from Romare Bearden Park in Uptown

COST Ticket prices start at $14 per game

PRO TIP Not in the mood for baseball? You can see into the ballpark and catch a glimpse of the dragon from nearby streets and Romare Bearden Park.

The next time you're cheering on the Charlotte Knights baseball team at BB&T stadium, head to the outfield to see this smoke-breathing dragon up-close and personal.

    Prefer a friendlier dragon for your game watching? Look for the Knights fuzzy Homer the Dragon mascot at the game. He once set a world record for "Most Hugs Given by a Mascot in a Twenty-four-hour Span."

8 THE HILTON SISTERS

Why is a pair of British conjoined twins buried in Charlotte?

On February 5, 1908, sisters Daisy and Violet Hilton were born in Brighton, England. They were joined at the hips and buttocks, sharing blood circulation, but no major organs. Their mother was an unmarried barmaid and her employer took the girls from her, seeing potential for making money by using them as entertainment.

The pair began touring as early as 1911, when they were only three years old. In 1926 they even performed a tap-dancing routine as part of an act with Bob Hope. Tragically, the twins were essentially held captive and abused by their managers until 1931 when the girls sued their managers and gained their freedom.

At that point, the Hiltons began touring in vaudeville acts and then burlesque venues. They each married different men, both of whom were known to be gay, and neither marriage lasted long. Violet and Daisy starred in films about their lives, and since their death they've been portrayed in a Broadway musical and an award-winning documentary.

While the Hilton sisters died in 1969, Forest Lawn West Cemetery where they are buried is still active with graves being added. Their grave is in a fairly nondescript area toward the back of the cemetery and just a few rows in from the road.

The conjoined Hilton twins, who were originally born in England, died tragically in Charlotte and share this grave at the picturesque Forest Lawn West Cemetery just outside of town.

In the 1960s, the Hiltons made their last public appearance at a drive-in in Charlotte. After that, in order to support themselves, they ended up working in a local grocery store. In 1969, the Hiltons died in their home of the Hong Kong flu. Today, you can see their grave at Forest Lawn West Cemetery off Freedom Drive in Charlotte.

FOREST LAWN WEST CEMETERY

WHAT A cemetery just outside of Uptown Charlotte

WHERE 4601 Freedom Dr.

COST Free

PRO TIP There are two other notable graves in the cemetery: Paul Campbell, a major league baseball player who played with the Boston Red Sox was buried here in 2006, and Olympic athlete, actor, and Purple Heart recipient Floyd "Chunk" Simmons was buried here in 2008.

9 NEED FOR SPEED

Where can you drive 140 mph (legally)?

NASCAR has a rich history in Charlotte. Its origins can be found during Prohibition, when drivers would run bootleg whiskey down from the Appalachian Mountains and into the region using small and fast cars to outrun the police. And while Prohibition ended in 1933, North Carolinians had developed a taste for moonshine and many of the drivers continued to "run 'shine" in their modified cars.

Today's version of the sport is, of course, a multibillion-dollar business, and Charlotte is home to both the NASCAR Hall of Fame and one of the sport's most impressive tracks. The Charlotte Motor Speedway, which was built in 1959, features a 1.5-mile track with turns banked at twenty-four degrees. It hosts the Coca-Cola 600 and the Bank of America 500 among other prestigious races.

And for those craving their own chance to get behind the wheel, the Speedway offers a Racing Experience. Its most popular version lasts three hours and includes an eight-minute racing session on the speedway with the chance to go up to 140 miles per hour.

For a more panoramic view of the impressive track, make reservations at the Speedway Club Restaurant. Open year-round for lunch and dinner, the upscale restaurant above the stands offers a sweeping view of the speedway.

Always dreamed of seeing the Charlotte Motor Speedway from the driver's seat? Now you can take a spin—at 140 miles per hour.

CHARLOTTE MOTOR SPEEDWAY

WHAT The NASCAR Driving Experience at the Speedway

WHERE 5555 Concord Pkwy., in Concord, NC, just outside of Charlotte

COST Prices vary, but the most popular package is $320

PRO TIP You'll need to be able to drive a stick shift for this and you must be small enough to climb in and out of the driver's window (just like the pros).

10. GO FOR THE GOLD

Can you still pan for gold at the site of the United States' first gold mine?

In 1799, Conrad Reed discovered what he thought was a seventeen-pound yellow rock in the creek on his family's farm. For three years the family used the rock as a doorstop at their farmhouse until in 1802 a jeweler identified it as a large gold nugget, prompting Conrad's father, John Reed, to begin the country's first gold mine.

More gold continued to be discovered, including a twenty-eight-pound nugget found by a slave. And while mining in the South decreased after the Civil War and the last underground mining in the region ended in 1912, the gold fever left its mark on Charlotte. Today, the city pays homage to this history with things like the Gold Rush Trolley system.

Those who want to see up-close where it started—and try their own hand at mining—can visit the Reed Mine. It's a state historic site with a museum as well as restored mine tunnels. And from April through the end of October guests to the mine can channel Conrad Reed and pan for gold themselves.

REED GOLD MINE

WHAT A historic gold mine northeast of Charlotte

WHERE 9621 Reed Mine Rd. in Midland, NC, about half an hour outside Charlotte

COST Admission is free and it's $3 per pan

PRO TIP Even on warm days, it can be cool in the underground mines. It's refreshing in the summer, but consider bringing additional clothing if you're going to explore on winter days.

At Reed Gold Mine just outside of Charlotte, guests can explore the underground tunnels of the country's first documented mine—and during some months even pan for their own gold on site.

The story of Reed Gold Mine is that when Reed's original gold nugget was identified as gold, he sold it for $3.50, not understanding its true value, which would have been closer to $3,600 at the time. In today's currency, it would be valued at around $250,000.

11 SCOOP OF HISTORY

Where can you enjoy a soft-serve cone with a side of Americana?

On the 2700 block of the busy Wilkinson Boulevard to the west of town you'll find the oldest location in North Carolina of the popular Dairy Queen ice cream chain. The first Dairy Queen ever opened in 1940 in Joliet, Illinois, and in the booming post-war years the chain had grown to 100 stores by 1947, when this one was built. (The location on Central Avenue is only three years younger, having been built in 1950.)

In addition to its art deco style and classic blue and white awning, this Diary Queen stands out as it has what is said to be the only remaining Dairy Queen Eskimo sign in existence. The woman, with white fur wrapped around her head, sits atop the restaurant holding an oversized ice cream cone.

Today, this is both a Charlotte historic site and a place where you can satisfy your Dairy Queen cravings from hot dogs to Dilly Bars. And its current owner keeps the sign maintained and freshly painted, ensuring you'll be able to indulge in both ice cream and history for years to come.

In addition to its "Dairy Queen" on top, the restaurant's architecture is historic art deco style. It features rounded front corners, square blue and white tiles in front of the serving windows, and a blue and white aluminum awning.

DAIRY QUEEN

WHAT A historic location of the famed ice cream chain

WHERE 2732 Wilkinson Blvd., just west of Uptown

COST Food prices vary and the menu can be found at www.dairyqueen.com

PRO TIP This location is just a few miles from the airport, making it the perfect first stop for out-of-town guests to enjoy a taste of Charlotte culture.

This Dairy Queen on Wilkinson Boulevard was built in 1947. It's the oldest in the state and features a retro eskimo holding an ice cream cone on top.

12 HOME OF THE HORNETS

What kinds of sports have the Charlotte Hornets played?

In the fall of 1780 the British army, led by General Cornwallis, arrived in Charlotte—but they only stayed 16 days. Later Cornwallis would say that it was because of the local patriots. He called Charlotte a "Hornet's Nest of Rebellion."

Charlotte embraced its "Hornet's nest" nickname and more than one hundred years later, the first local team under the name was the Charlotte Hornets baseball team, which came up to bat in 1892. They played under that name until 1937, and after going through a series of other names, they're now known as the Charlotte Knights.

In 1974, the Charlotte Hornets became the city's first major league football team when they relocated here from New York City and played at American Legion Memorial Stadium. But this didn't last long, with the team ending operations in 1975.

Ten years later, the Charlotte Hornets basketball team took to the court as the city's first NBA team. In 2002, the

---

If you're a fan of the current Charlotte Hornets, check out the Hornets Fan Shop on the bottom level of Uptown's Spectrum Center—known as The Hive. You'll find plenty of items for game day as well as fun accessories for your home or office, showing your support for the home team.

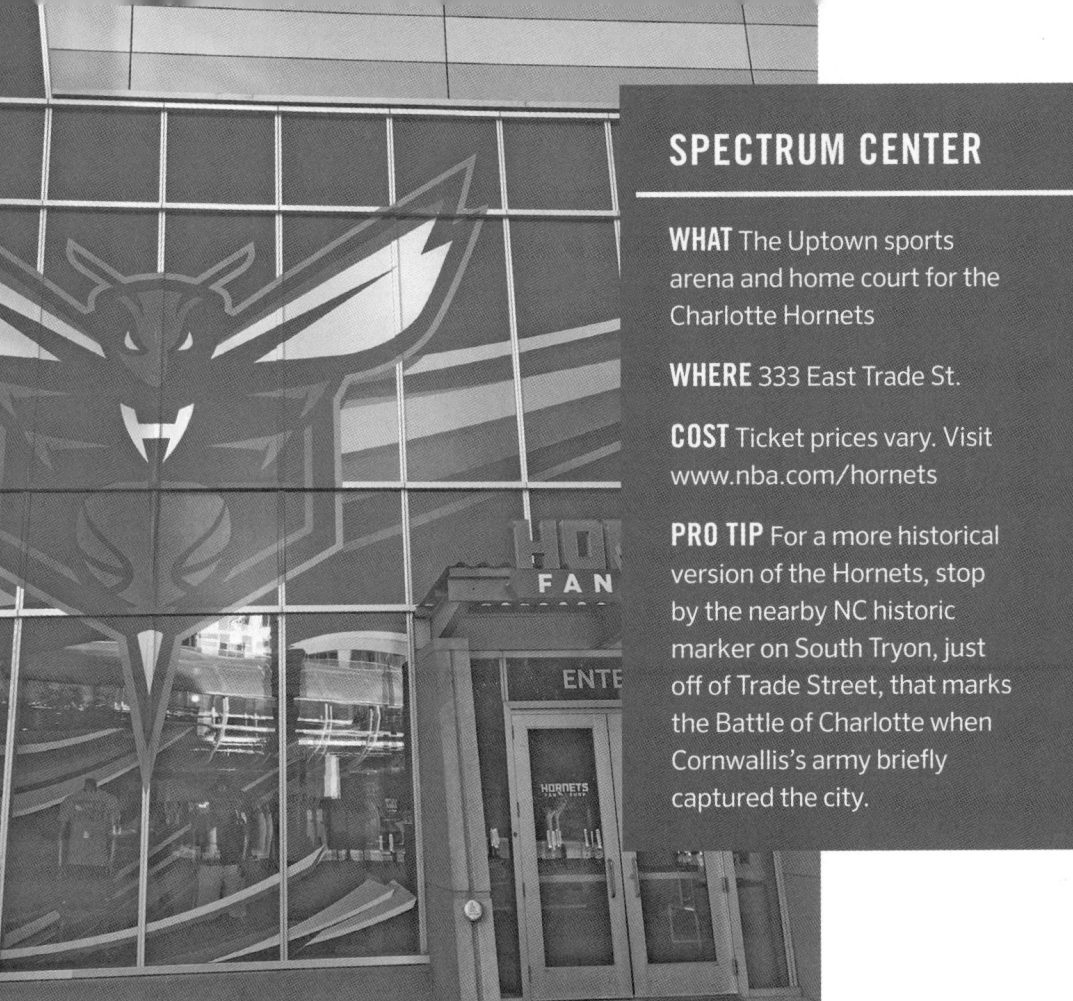

SPECTRUM CENTER

WHAT The Uptown sports arena and home court for the Charlotte Hornets

WHERE 333 East Trade St.

COST Ticket prices vary. Visit www.nba.com/hornets

PRO TIP For a more historical version of the Hornets, stop by the nearby NC historic marker on South Tryon, just off of Trade Street, that marks the Battle of Charlotte when Cornwallis's army briefly captured the city.

While the Hornets has been the name for many sports teams in Charlotte, today it's the name of the city's NBA basketball team, which plays in Spectrum Arena.

team moved to New Orleans and in 2004 the Charlotte Bobcats were born. But Charlotte missed its Hornets. (One might even say the city was a "Hornet's Nest of Rebellion" in regards to wanting its NBA team name back.) And so in 2014 the New Orleans Hornets were renamed the Pelicans and today Charlotte can once again cheer on its home team Hornets.

13 MINT CONDITION

Why is Charlotte's most renowned museum named the Mint Museum?

Now known as a banking center, Charlotte has a long and storied past when it comes to money. In 1837, the Charlotte Mint opened in Uptown on the 400 block of West Trade Street, producing what are now extremely rare coins like the $2.50 quarter eagles. Ultimately, in addition to processing raw gold, the Mint created more than $5 million in gold currency.

After North Carolina seceded from the Union during the Civil War, the Confederate government took over the Mint, initially continuing business as usual. But as the war progressed, the space was turned into a hospital and military office. Following the war, coinage never resumed, but the building served a variety of purposes including being a Red Cross station during World War I and a meeting place for the Charlotte Women's Club.

While the Randolph Road location of the Mint Museum is its original location, today it's the less visited of the two Mint Museums. The Uptown version of the Mint, which opened on South Tryon Street in 2010, features 145,000 square feet of galleries and gathering areas over five floors.

At the Mint Museum on Randolph Road you can see hints of the museum's storied past as a United States mint, such as the gold eagle above its entrance.

MINT MUSEUM RANDOLPH

WHAT The original location of the Mint Museum of Art

WHERE 2730 Randolph Rd. in the Eastover neighborhood of Charlotte

COST General admission for adults is $12 and includes admission to the Mint Museum Uptown within a two-day period

PRO TIP Check out the Heritage Gallery, which tells the story of the museum's past. And if you're looking to save a little of your own money while learning about the museum's history with money, visit between 5 and 9 p.m. on a Wednesday night, when admission is free.

In 1931, the Charlotte Mint building was set to be demolished, but a group of local citizens obtained it and relocated it to the site of a former dairy farm on Randolph Road. There it became the state's first art museum, the Mint Museum of Art, holding its inaugural exhibit in 1936. Today, in addition to its arts and crafts, visitors to this museum can enjoy the historic building—and its extensive coin collection from the original Mint.

14 BREAKING THE BANK

What makes the 1997 robbery in Charlotte one of the most notorious heists in recent history?

On the night of October 4, 1997, a vault supervisor at a regional armored-car warehouse of Loomis, Fargo & Co. just outside of Uptown Charlotte stole $17.3 million with the help of his girlfriend and six others. At the time, it was the second-largest cash robbery to happen in the United States—but what makes it especially well known are the cast of characters involved, whose use of the stolen money earned the robbery the nickname the "Hillbilly Heist."

David Scott Ghantt, the vault supervisor who initially took the money, was caught on videotape removing it and loading it into a van. He and two other co-conspirators abandoned the van in nearby woods, leaving $3.3 million inside because they'd miscalculated how much space the currency would actually take up.

While the Loomis Fargo Heist happened on Suttle Avenue just to the west of Uptown Charlotte, the recent big budget comedic film depicting the robbery—and starring Zach Galifianakis—was actually filmed in the Asheville, North Carolina, area.

LOOMIS ARMORED US

WHAT The location of the famed 1997 heist

WHERE 2050 Suttle Ave., just to the east of Uptown Charlotte

COST Not open to the public

PRO TIP You won't gain much from seeing the location. Those who want to learn more should purchase former *Charlotte Observer* reporter Jeff Diamant's book *Heist!: The $17 Million Loomis Fargo Theft*. Or, for the more amusing, but not as factually accurate version, watch the story in *Masterminds* starring Zach Galifianakis.

Today, the location of the famed Loomis Fargo heist that has inspired books and movies is a warehouse that's being rented by a local church. But security cameras around the building and parking lot tell the story of its past.

Ghantt ran for Mexico with $50,000 while those left behind began quickly spending their shares. They moved from mobile homes into mansions and purchased things like a tanning bed, a velvet Elvis painting, and breast implants. This, of course, ultimately attracted the attention of the FBI, who arrested and charged all involved.

15 PARK OF THE PAST

What ever happened to Heritage USA theme park?

When Jim and Tammy Faye Bakker founded the Christian theme park Heritage USA in Fort Mill in 1978, the couple was in their heyday as the televangelists with the PTL Club (short for "Praise the Lord"). Initially, the park thrived, bringing in more than $100 million annually as people visited its hotel, Main Street USA, skating rink, studios, school, and waterpark. It was the third-most visited theme park in the country behind Disney World and Disneyland.

Things began to go wrong for the park when, in the late 1980s, the IRS revoked its tax exemption. Then things quickly got worse as Jim Bakker resigned from the ministry following a sex scandal and was imprisoned for accounting fraud. Ultimately, Hurricane Hugo damaged many of the buildings and in 1989 the complex officially closed.

Today, MorningStar Fellowship Church meets in the atrium-style lobby of what was Jim Bakker's Heritage Grand Hotel. MorningStar Ministries owns 52 acres around the hotel, as well as the conference center. When they purchased the property in 2004, it was in a state of disrepair, but the church continues to work to restore it.

While Heritage USA theme park was once known as a happy place filled with families and children, today the area is partially abandoned and rundown.

HERITAGE USA

WHAT The crumbling ruins of the former theme park

WHERE Take exit 90 off I-77 and drive one mile down Carowinds Blvd. to a parking lot with the unfinished tower on one side and the park on the other

COST The park is not open to the public, but visitors are welcome for free at the restored Upper Room

PRO TIP There's an overgrown chain-link fence, but if you look through you can see the lake that was once the center of the park. Behind the tower you'll find MorningStar Ministries, another evangelical group that owns much of the former site. The Upper Room, which was once part of Heritage USA, has reopened on the site as a place of prayer.

Today, much of the twenty-three-hundred-acre park has been demolished, including the King's Castle, which was bulldozed in 2013. But there are still reminders of the past like miniature railroad tracks and the halfway-finished twenty-one-story tower. There are some religious-focused parts though that have been restored and are once again open to visitors, including the "Upper Room," which is said to replicate the Jerusalem room of Jesus' Last Supper.

16 TOAST TO TREEHOUSES

Why are there treehouses in a Charlotte vineyard?

North Carolina isn't known for its vineyards—yet. In recent years the state's wine production has taken off, with vineyards popping up primarily around the Yadkin Valley region.

But just outside of Charlotte is a different sort of vineyard. The picturesque property is comprised of rolling hills of muscadine vines, all of which are best viewed from one of its oversized treehouses. Phil and Dianne Nordan planted the vineyard in 2004, but Phil had already built his first treehouse on the site in 1999. The Eastern North Carolina native had grown up building treehouses and thought it would be fun to build one for adults.

Today, that first treehouse is thirty feet above the ground with steep stairs leading up to it, and it features views of the vineyard and is perfect for enjoying the sunset from one of its rocking chairs. Both treehouses on the vineyard

---

The treehouses aren't the only things that make this Monroe vineyard playful. Its wines come with amusing stories and names like Tack Shack Red, Just One More Thing, and Liquid Sunshine. You'll hear the full story behind each name at the tastings, which are $6 and performed each hour.

At this picturesque vineyard in Monroe it's possible to rent out treehouses, both by the hour for a glass of wine while the sunsets or by the night for a playful evening spent among the limbs.

are available for rental (one for overnight stays) and offer an unusual twist on a trip to taste wines.

TREEHOUSE VINEYARDS

WHAT A vineyard just outside of Charlotte known for its playful treehouses

WHERE 301 Bay St., Monroe, NC

COST Tastings are $6 per person and include a flight of wines and the stories behind them

PRO TIP The Date Nite Treehouse is actually perfect for small groups and can hold up to six adults. Reserve it online before you go (it's $25 per hour). The vineyard's shop sells both wines and snacks for you to enjoy during your time in the trees.

17 PARANORMAL ACTIVITY

Do people summon the ghosts of slaves at this Charlotte home?

Just north of Uptown Charlotte is Historic Rosedale Plantation. The forty-six-hundred-square-foot home, which now sits on 8.5 acres, was built on more than nine hundred acres in 1815. In addition to its owners through the years, the plantation was also home to several slave families.

Today, the home, which was built by Archibald Frew and once called "Frew's Folly" (possibly for its bright yellow trim and over-the-top opulence), is open to visitors. And while regular guided tours of the home are available year-round, October features several especially popular tours and events.

On the "Spirits of Rosedale Plantation" tour, guests learn the stories of former—and possibly current—inhabitants like a slave named Cherry who is said to haunt the basement kitchen. For a seriously spooky evening there's a Paranormal Grounds Investigation that includes professional ghost hunters attempting contact with the beyond throughout

---

If ghostly visits aren't your thing, consider checking out Historic Rosedale Plantation another time. The home is decorated in period style at Christmas and its gardens are especially beautiful during the spring. The best time to visit, though, may be for its annual Feast of the Hunter's Moon dinner in the fall.

While Historic Rosedale Plantation looks beautiful by daylight, on nights in October ghost hunters search for paranormal activity in and around the old home.

HISTORIC ROSEDALE PLANTATION

WHAT A more than two-hundred-year-old plantation home in Charlotte

WHERE 3427 N Tryon St., Charlotte

COST Tour prices vary, but start at $15 per person for the spooky versions

PRO TIP While the Spirits of Rosedale tour is playful and theatrical, making it fun for children over six, the other ghost hunting tours are designed for adults.

the home's four floors. And for the ultimate ghostly experience, there's an event at midnight in the home's garden, with staff and volunteers sharing their encounters and scary experiences before attempting to contact the spirits.

18 BUG ON A BUILDING

Why is a Volkswagen Beetle permanently parked on the roof of a popular burger joint?

You may have seen Pinky's Westside Grill on the famed Food Network show *Diners, Drive-Ins, and Dives*. Its chef, Greg Auten, was the first person to appear on the popular show twice when he was featured on Season 1 for the then-popular (and since closed) Penguin Drive-In, where he was chef and co-owner, and then again in Season 22 for Pinky's Westside Grill, which he launched as both chef and owner.

And while Auten is known for his tasty fried pickle chips and creative hot dogs and burgers, the first thing that catches your eye at this spot won't be on the menu. Because it's housed in a former auto shop, the building features a red, white, and blue 1966 Volkswagen Beetle on its roof. The current owners fought to keep the car there—something it turned out they were smart to do. Today, the colorful bug has become iconic in the fast-growing, trendy neighborhood.

Pinky's isn't the only restaurant in the newly dubbed FreeMoreWest neighborhood with a colorful history. Just down the street is the Open Kitchen, a restaurant that opened in the 1950s and proclaims itself to be home to the area's first pizza pie.

Formerly an auto shop, the popular Pinky's restaurant features this colorfully decorated VW Bug on its roof, making it a notable local landmark.

PINKY'S WESTSIDE GRILL

WHAT A popular, casual burger bar housed in a former auto shop

WHERE 1600 W Morehead St., Charlotte

COST Prices vary for food and drinks, but are in the inexpensive range

PRO TIP Order Greg's Pickles. The warm, fried dill pickle chips are served with a cool ranch dressing, and are famous for good reason.

19 COMING UP ROSES

Why is there a full-size coal train car tucked in of one of the city's most beautiful gardens?

In 1950, one of Charlotte's leading philanthropists, Henry McGill, purchased the Avant Fuel & Ice Company on a plot of land near the train tracks on North Davidson Street, just outside of Uptown. His wife, Helen, felt that the urban and industrial area needed something beautiful, and so she began to plant rose bushes along the fence.

As the years passed, more and more rose bushes were planted until the garden had more than five hundred bushes covering almost two acres. In 1962, the garden opened to the public for the first time on Mother's Day. Then, in 1975, the coal and ice yard closed and the property was sold to the City of Charlotte to be turned into a public park.

Today, it's a nonprofit garden and open to the public with free admission. And those who choose to wander its paths will find fountains, benches, and more than a thousand fragrant rose bushes, as well as a nod to its not-so-beautiful past: a full-sized coal car still sitting in the corner of the garden atop a piece of railroad track.

If a stroll through the gorgeous gardens has you wishing for fresh cut florals to take home, you're in the right place. Nectar, a boutique flower shop, is located adjacent to the garden. The stylish flower shop creates bouquets for any occasion and even has a mobile flower truck.

McGill Rose Garden is an unexpected treasure for anyone who has made their way from the busy and industrial North Davidson Street into its blooming and fragrant paths. And within it is one more unexpected find: an old coal train car.

MCGILL ROSE GARDEN

WHAT A public garden filled with hundreds of rose bushes

WHERE 940 N Davidson St., Charlotte

COST Admission to the garden is free

PRO TIP Blooming season typically goes from late April into November, but the best time to visit the garden is generally in mid-May when many of the gorgeous and colorful bushes are in bloom.

20 UP IS DOWN

Why do Charlotteans call their downtown Uptown?

There's much debate in Charlotte on this subject, but one thing is for sure: For the last several decades, it has been accepted that the center city area of Charlotte is called Uptown rather than downtown. It's something that confuses outsiders, and is an easy way to identify a newcomer.

There are two historical reasons commonly pointed to for this difference. The first is that Charlotte was founded at the intersection of two Native American trading paths, which are today Trade and Tryon Streets. That intersection was the highest elevation point in town and so when people went there, they were literally going up.

More recently, in 1974 a local merchant pushed for a city council proclamation declaring that center city be officially called "Uptown" in order to give positive associations for its businesses. According to the merchant, the area had been called Uptown in the 1950s and it needed to return to that designation. Regardless of its origins, the nomenclature has stuck. Charlotteans are firm in saying that the city doesn't have a downtown—only an Uptown.

If a walking tour of Charlotte's Uptown doesn't sound exciting, try a different version. Visitors to Uptown can take Segway tours or carriage rides, or for an at-your-own-pace version, take the Charlotte Liberty Walk to fifteen historic sites around town.

Charlotte's skyline actually sits on a hill, which may be one of the reasons locals call it Uptown. But the main reason for calling center city Uptown? It sounds more positive.

UPTOWN CHARLOTTE

WHAT The central area of Charlotte, marked in its middle by the intersection of Tryon and Trade Streets

WHERE This area of town is broken into four wards and is surrounded by I-277 and I-77

COST Free

PRO TIP To learn about Uptown's history—including where it got its name—book a Center City Walking Tour with Charlotte NC Tours (www.charlottenctours.com). It includes a look at modern Charlotte and a narration of the city's history from the mid-1700s.

21 MAKING MAGIC

Did David Copperfield get blown up in a Charlotte landmark as part of a magic trick?

The answer to this question is: Well, not exactly, but it certainly looked like it to thousands of viewers on national television.

In 1988, the DH Griffin Wrecking Company was set to tear down one of Uptown's most notable buildings. Hotel Charlotte, which opened in 1924 on the site of what is now the Carillon building at 231 W Trade Street, had hosted guests from Elvis to Franklin D. Roosevelt. But as development moved to the suburbs, the hotel had ultimately closed its doors in the 1970s. And after sitting empty for more than a decade, it was scheduled for demolition.

That's when CBS stepped in. The network wanted to film "The Magic of David Copperfield XI: The Explosive Encounter" in Charlotte. In the episode, Copperfield would be locked in a safe inside the building with two and a half minutes to escape before the hotel imploded.

Before his death in 1991, Jean Tinguely, who created the Cascade sculpture that hangs inside the Carillon building, was married to Niki de Saint Phalle, the French artist, behind the Bechtler Museum of Modern Art's iconic Firebird sculpture.

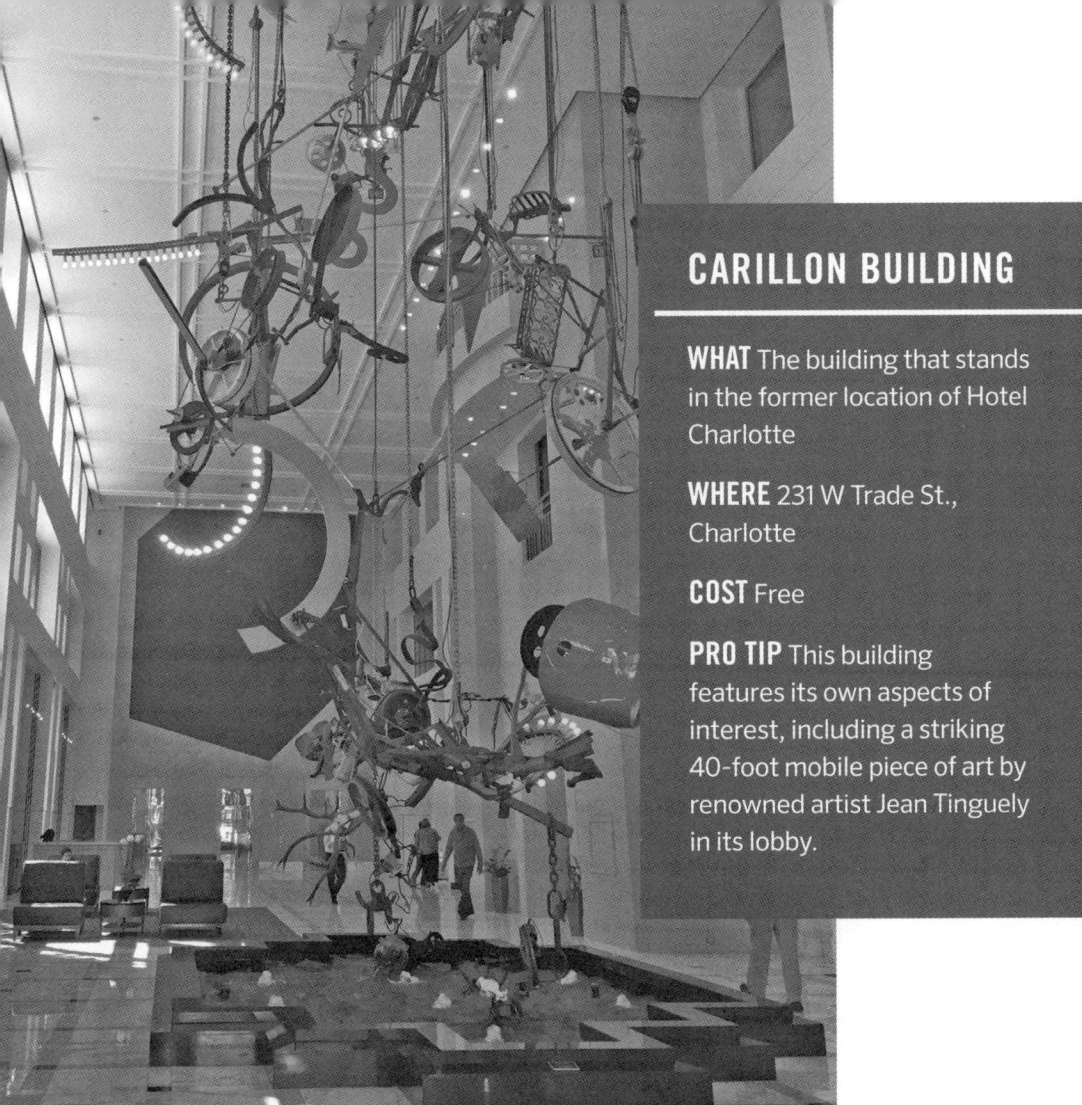

Before the Carillon Tower was built as a home to businesses, up-scale condos, and a Jean Tinguely mobile masterpiece, the famed Hotel Charlotte was on this site.

CARILLON BUILDING

WHAT The building that stands in the former location of Hotel Charlotte

WHERE 231 W Trade St., Charlotte

COST Free

PRO TIP This building features its own aspects of interest, including a striking 40-foot mobile piece of art by renowned artist Jean Tinguely in its lobby.

The footage, which aired in 1989, made it appear as though Copperfield's magic was a success. And while according to participants the "magic" was the result of some expert camera work and a false back on the safe, it was ultimately an exciting end to what had been one of Charlotte's most colorful destinations.

22 HERE'S A TIP

Where can you find a tip jar made from a prosthetic leg?

Puckett's Farm Equipment has been a part of north Charlotte's Derita neighborhood for more than eighty years. And while it originally sold tractors, after Prohibition ended, the country store started to sell beer. As farming in the region slowed, the farmers began to gather more often to share a beer—and their sorrows at the dying local industry. These days, the tractors aren't around, but the grandson of the original owner is still selling beer and now this popular bar offers live music.

The spot, which features a stage and sound system, has hosted a variety of live music performers from around the region, even including The Avett Brothers before they made it big. Most of the music is country and bluegrass, with the bar pegging itself as a "21st-Century Honky Tonk."

And while having a music venue inside a former tractor sales store might already feel strange, what really sets the eclectic Puckett's apart is its tip jar. Standing on the stage in front of the band area is a solo prosthetic leg. Want to tip the performers? Drop your cash inside.

PUCKETT'S FARM EQUIPMENT

WHAT A laid-back bar just north of town

WHERE 2740 W Sugar Creek Rd. (at the intersection of Mallard Creek Rd.)

COST Admission is free and the beer is inexpensive

PRO TIP Weekend nights are best for a visit, when local musicians take the stage. But if you're looking to try your own hand at the tunes and tips, visit for open mic on Monday nights.

At a bar and music venue named Puckett's Farm Equipment, nothing should come as a surprise. But this tip jar made from a prosthetic leg may still catch your eye.

If you're looking for a music venue and bar, it's easy to miss Puckett's Farm Equipment as you drive by on Sugar Creek Road. Located across from a shopping center, the only indication that the brick building is no longer only selling tractors is a small "Pub" sign by its front door.

23. THE MILL DEAL

Where can you see a scale once used to weigh cotton—while you drink wine?

Chances are, you've been to Atherton Mill and Market. The historic South End mill has been revitalized in recent years to include some of the city's hottest new restaurants and retail. But this mill has a long history prior to becoming a dining and shopping destination.

Opened in 1893, the mill was owned by Daniel Augustus Tompkins, who would ultimately build more than one hundred cotton mills around the southern U.S. Tomkins lived in Charlotte and chose the Atherton location because of the city's railroads, one of which ran next to the mill.

The textile mill, which included a mill village of around fifty cottages and a school on the nearby Dilworth blocks, was a loud space with noisy machines producing the yarn. It was one of the first mills to incorporate construction to prevent the spread of flames in fires, but it was a dangerous environment and many of its workers were children.

Daniel Augustus Tompkins, who originally opened Atherton Mill, is credited with being one of Charlotte's major developers and leaders. In addition to building more than 100 cotton mills around the Southeast, he owned the Charlotte Daily Observer newspaper and wrote books on textiles.

ATHERTON MILL AND MARKET

WHAT A cotton mill turned shopping and dining destination

WHERE 2000 South Blvd., Charlotte

COST Free

PRO TIP Look for the old trolley car tracks on the west side of the mill and be sure to stop in Vin Master Wine to see some of the building's original architecture—and, of course, sample the wine.

Atherton Mill, which was once a large textile mill, is now filled with shops and restaurants. Stop in Vin Master to see a scale that used to weigh cotton at the historic mill.

    The mill operated as Atherton Cotton Mills until the 1920s when it became simply Atherton Mills. Then, in the 1930s it became a candy and baked goods factory until the 1960s. Today, you can still peek into the past if you stop in the Vin Master wine shop and bar, which was once the mill's loading dock. Look for the original floor-to-ceiling windows as well as a large scale that was used to weigh cotton—and still works today.

24 SYMBOLIC STATUES

What do the sculptures in Charlotte's center mean?

Smack in the middle of Uptown Charlotte you'll find the intersection of Trade and Tryon Streets. On the four corners of the intersection are four large bronze statues. The statues, which were dedicated in 1995, were designed by sculptor Ramond Kaskey, who also designed the Queen Charlotte statue at Charlotte Douglas Airport.

Each statue weighs close to five thousand pounds and stands around twenty-five-feet tall. And each one represents different elements of Charlotte: commerce, industry, transportation, and the future.

Commerce is depicted by a prospector holding a gold pan, giving a nod to Charlotte's first gold rush. *Industry* is a female millworker with a child, representing the many women and children who worked in the area's mills.

While at first glance these sculptures appear fairly simple, there are intricate details on each one. For example, look for the number 1401 on the transportation statue, which refers to the Southern Railway steam engine 1401 that ran through Charlotte. Or look closely at the Commerce statue—just below his pan you'll see the face of former Federal Reserve Chairman Alan Greenspan.

INDEPENDENCE SQUARE

WHAT The square in the center of the city features several public works of art

WHERE Intersection of Trade and Tryon Streets

COST Free

PRO TIP Look closely at the sculptures for symbolic details. For example, the *Future* sculpture features dogwood branches (the state tree of North Carolina) with a hornets' nest (a historic symbol of Charlotte).

It's easy to walk right past the four sculptures around the square at Trade and Tryon Streets in the center of the city. But pause to look closely at them to spot details that are nods to the Queen City.

Transportation is an African American man meant to represent the builders of the area's first railroads. And finally, *Future* shows a mother with her child, indicating the city's hope for new life.

49

25. HOME SWEET HOME

Why are there Victorian mansions in Uptown's historic Fourth Ward neighborhood?

These days, skyscrapers and modern architecture take up most of Charlotte's center city. Its historic homes and buildings have been long since demolished, in large part as a result of the government's Urban Renewal program in the 1950s and 1960s, which was designed to remove unsightly low-income housing. Unfortunately, in addition to pushing out the vibrant culture of the city's lower income communities, the program also cleared out many of the area's more impressive homes.

Then, in the 1970s, the focus shifted—right around the same time it became popular to renovate historic Victorian homes. And while the city's master plan from 1966 indicated that the historic residences in the Fourth Ward should be bulldozed in favor of more skyscrapers, local Charlotteans saw the value in preserving some of these homes and through them, the city's history.

Redevelopment began in the neighborhood in the late 1970s and now around forty of the several hundred houses

---

In addition to its blocks of Victorian houses, Fourth Ward is also home to a picturesque three-acre urban park. Tucked into the historic neighborhood, the park features walking trails, fountains, and unusual planting like flowering apricot trees and weeping Japanese maple.

Uptown's Fourth Ward is like no other neighborhood in town. Filled with historic homes just steps away from the city's skyscrapers the neighborhood feels like it belongs in another city.

HISTORIC FOURTH WARD

WHAT The neighborhood in the northwest quadrant of Uptown Charlotte featuring one-hundred-plus-year-old Victorian homes

WHERE The area is loosely bordered by Graham St., 10th St., Church St., and 6th St.

COST Free

PRO TIP There are walking maps for touring the area available at Charlotte's Visitor Information Center at 501 S College St. Keep an eye out for annual tours including a holiday tour in December and garden tour in May. And whenever you go, plan on stopping in for a bite at Alexander Michael's. A local tavern located in the former Crowell-Berryhill grocery store, which opened in 1897, Al Mike's has been a neighborhood favorite since the area's redevelopment in the early 1980s.

originally there, remain in its historic district. A walk down its tree-lined streets will take you past Victorian-style homes from the late 1800s, including an 1890s residence on Church Street where Charlotte mayor S.S. McNinch lived at one time. Like its neighbors, it's an impressive home that especially stands out against the backdrop of the rest of the city's gleaming high-rises.

26 UNDER WATER

What's beneath the surface of Lake Norman?

If you've just driven by or spent an afternoon on a boat on the pristine waters of Lake Norman, chances are you didn't think much about what's below the surface. The man-made lake, just to the north of Charlotte, features 520 miles of shoreline that are more than enough to keep your attention above the waterline.

But what is beneath the water offers plenty of its own stories. The lake was created in 1963, when Duke Energy flooded hundreds of acres with water from the Catawba River—and many of those acres had previously held homes, businesses, and even cemeteries.

One of the most notable homes was Elm Wood Estate, a Georgian-style plantation house built by a Revolutionary War General in the 1820s. Part of the home had been dismantled in an attempt to move it, but that project was abandoned and today much of the plantation house is beneath the waters of the lake.

There was one other unusual thing recently found beneath the lake's surface. In 2013, a plane was found in ninety feet of water when the Charlotte Fire Department's dive team was doing practice drills. According to the Federal Aviation Administration, the plane had been there since the summer of 1974.

RAMSEY CREEK PARK

WHAT Lake Norman's public beach

WHERE 18441 Nantz Rd., Cornelius

COST $3 parking

PRO TIP Sure, you won't be able to spy the treasures beneath the surface of the lake from this picturesque park and beach, but it's a nice spot to spend an afternoon imagining what lies beneath.

While the view from the public beach at Ramsey Creek Park makes Lake Norman appear pristine, its waters cover structures ranging from mills to mansions.

Two cotton mills, which were both owned by Duke Energy, had been closed for several years before the lake was formed. The mills were both large, employing more than one hundred people each, and were surrounded by mill villages. Today, many of the village homes, as well as the mills—and even some of the large machinery in the mills—still rest below the lake's surface.

Duke Energy was very careful about removing one thing though. Every grave that was in the path of the lake's formation was carefully moved to dry land, resulting in at least seven family cemeteries being moved out of the lake's path.

27 DC IN NC

Why is there an exact replica of a Washington Senatorial office in Monroe?

Jesse Helms was a five-term U.S. Senator from North Carolina, making him the longest-serving popularly elected Senator in the state's history. Helms, who was born in Monroe, just outside of Charlotte, was in office until 2003—and was well known both for his conservative politics and his often controversial comments.

In 1988, when Helms was still in office, he gave the go-ahead for the creation of the Jesse Helms Center in Wingate. Today, the center features archives of the late Senator, such as speeches and correspondence, as well as an interactive museum dedicated to his time in office.

But perhaps the most noteworthy part of the exhibit is the exact replica of Senator Helms' former office in the Dirksen Building on DC's Capitol Hill. The office features plaques covering its walls, a North Carolina flag in the corner, a small television, and family photos, all around a large oak desk. And look for the stamp on top of his desk. Senator Helms was well known as an obstructionist and enjoyed his nickname "Senator No." On his desk you'll find his famed large "No" rubber stamp.

At the Jesse Helms' Center in Wingate you'll find a variety of the late senator's papers and political materials. But possibly the most fascinating aspect of the exhibit is the exact replica of his Washington, DC, office.

THE JESSE HELMS CENTER

WHAT A private museum dedicated to the late Senator Jesse Helms

WHERE 3910 US Hwy 74, Wingate, NC

COST Admission is free

PRO TIP The center is home to hundreds of letters and photographs from the Senator. One of the more interesting that you'll want to check out is the correspondence between Senator Helms and Chelsea Clinton—when her father was in the White House.

The Jesse Helms Center is considered an interactive museum and offers free, self-guided tours throughout the week. It also features a twenty-minute film called "Courage of His Convictions," which tells the story of the senator's life.

28 IT'S A SIGN

Why is there a sign in Uptown Charlotte pointing to Edgar, Wisconsin?

Tucked among Uptown's sky rises and cultural centers, you'll find The Green, a 1.5-acre park adjacent to St. Peter's Catholic Church. Filled with fountains and grassy areas, The Green is a favorite spot for Uptown workers on their lunch breaks and those just looking for a serene spot away from the city's bustle.

Traveling public sculptures are often showcased in the garden, including an exhibition by famed French artist Niki de Saint Phalle that brought five large sculptures there in 2011. But overall the park's theme is international literature. Bronze books are among the most noted modern sculptures in the garden and you'll find quotes from well-known authors throughout its verdant space.

But perhaps the most whimsical nods to literature are the direction signs throughout The Green that point to actual cities and, when combined, make the names of authors. (e.g., Edgar, Wisconsin, and Allan, Saskatchewan, and Poe, Alberta, create Edgar Allan Poe).

The Green, which is owned by Wells Fargo, is known as a pocket park. It's tucked between two museums, a historic urban church, and the Charlotte Convention Center, and beneath its lush grounds you'll find a convenient parking garage.

Take a stroll through Uptown's 1.5-acre Green where all of the art is dedicated to the theme of literature. In addition to arrows pointing to towns that make up names of famous authors, there are also quotes from well-known writers and large bronze books.

THE GREEN

WHAT A 1.5-acre park in Uptown Charlotte

WHERE 400 S Tryon St.

COST Free

PRO TIP Enjoying the art in this park? The Green is just across the street from the Bechtler Museum of Modern Art and the Mint Museum, if you'd like to see more of the city's top art offerings.

29 FROM CARS TO COLD WAR

Why were missiles once made just a few miles outside of Uptown Charlotte?

Charlotte's North End isn't exactly its most notable historical area. While revitalization is in the works, large swaths of the once industrial neighborhood have sat vacant for many years. But a drive north on Statesville Avenue will actually reveal an area rich with history.

One of the most interesting stories on this street is that of the Hercules Industrial Park, which was originally built in the 1920s as a Ford Assembly Plant creating Henry Ford's Model T cars. From 1924 to 1932, the plant manufactured more than two hundred thousand cars and trucks, but during the Depression business plummeted and ultimately production ceased.

Then, in the 1940s, following the Japanese attack at Pearl Harbor, the former plant was purchased to become the Army Quartermaster Depot. There, hundreds of locals

---

Before it was a warehouse or a missile plant or an army quartermaster depot, 1776 Statesville Avenue was built to be a Ford Motor Company Assembly Plant. Mule-drawn wagons and steam-powered cranes were used on its foundation, and the plant employed 500 local Charlotteans during its first year of business.

It doesn't look like much from the outside—and it's behind a tall, chain-link fence—but this building just to the north of Uptown has a deep history from assembling Model T Fords to making missiles.

STATESVILLE AVENUE WAREHOUSE

WHAT The former Ford Motor Plant and Army Missile Plant is currently being used primarily as a Rite Aid Warehouse

WHERE 1776 Statesville Ave. (at the intersection with Woodward Ave.)

COST This isn't open to the public, but you can catch a glimpse from the street

PRO TIP Albert Kahn, who built around 2,000 factories between 1900 and 1940, was the architect for the original plant. He's an important figure in the history of this industrial architectural period, and you'll notice interesting details on the building's exterior that set it apart from many of the area's former textile mills.

worked to process and distribute supplies during World War II.

But perhaps most notable among the building's many incarnations was its role as the Charlotte Army Missile Plant (CAMP) during the Cold War. It was one of only two plants in the country making missiles for the Nike Program, which was the country's primary air defense system at that time. And if being the only plant that made the Nike Hercules missile wasn't enough to intrigue you the next time you're on Statesville Avenue, consider that CAMP also worked on a rocket and aerospace vehicles for NASA.

30 ROAD OF SHARON

Why do so many Charlotte roads have Sharon as part of their name?

There was a humorous quip circulating at one point that naming so many roads around Charlotte some version of Sharon was actually part of a plan to grow the city—because no one would ever be able to find their way out of it. And while that doesn't seem to have any basis in truth, anyone who has come to the intersection of Sharon Road and Sharon View Road is still left with some questions.

The name actually comes from Charlotte's early settlers who were Scotch-Irish Presbyterians. They named Sharon Presbyterian Church after Sharon, a region in Israel referenced in the Bible. And at that time roads were named for the church to which they led. Enter Sharon Road and roads like Sharon Amity Road, which connects Sharon Presbyterian and Amity Presbyterian churches.

When the name really began to spread though was in the 1920s, after Governor Cameron Morrison built his home near Sharon Church. Suddenly, the name Sharon became a status symbol and other roads

---

SHARON PRESBYTERIAN CHURCH

WHAT A historic church that was founded in 1830

WHERE 5201 Sharon Rd.

COST Free

PRO TIP In addition to being one of the city's oldest churches, Sharon Presbyterian Church is also remembered in history for its ties to famed evangelist Billy Graham. At age nineteen Graham preached in this church where many of his relatives were members. His father was buried at the church for several years until his grave was moved to be interred alongside his wife at a different cemetery.

Many of Charlotte's roads were named for its churches, including the many variations of Sharon, which likely stemmed from the historic Sharon Presbyterian Church.

around town began popping up with the name. Today, you'll find more than a dozen variations of Sharon on our street signs—which is still confusing, but at least you'll know why.

Sharon Amity Road connected Sharon Presbyterian Church and Amity Presbyterian Church. The original Amity Presbyterian Church was erected in 1882 as a log structure and was only sixteen by twenty-four feet.

31 BIRD WATCHING

Why is there a giant sparkling chicken-like bird in Uptown Charlotte?

In front of Uptown's Bechtler Museum of Modern Art stands the glittering 17.5-foot-tall *Firebird* sculpture. Since its arrival at the museum in 2009, it's become one of the city's most photographed objects, with tourists and locals alike pausing to snap their photos beneath its oversized wings.

But there's more to the story of the *Firebird* than simply its photogenic qualities. It was created in 1991 by French-American artist Niki de Saint Phalle and had been on display around the world until Charlotte resident and Switzerland native Andreas Bechtler spotted it in an exhibit at the Atlanta Botanical Garden.

Bechtler, the museum's namesake and benefactor, knew it would be the perfect fit for the outdoor space. Not just because of its impressive looks, but because the museum was designed by architect Mario Botta. Botta had collaborated with de Saint Phalle in the past on projects, making her sculptures the perfect complement to his architecture.

The Bechtler Museum of Modern Art's Firebird Society supports the museum through donations and annual events. Each fall, the group holds a Firebird Anniversary celebration on the museum's plaza that features live depictions of the sparkling sculpture.

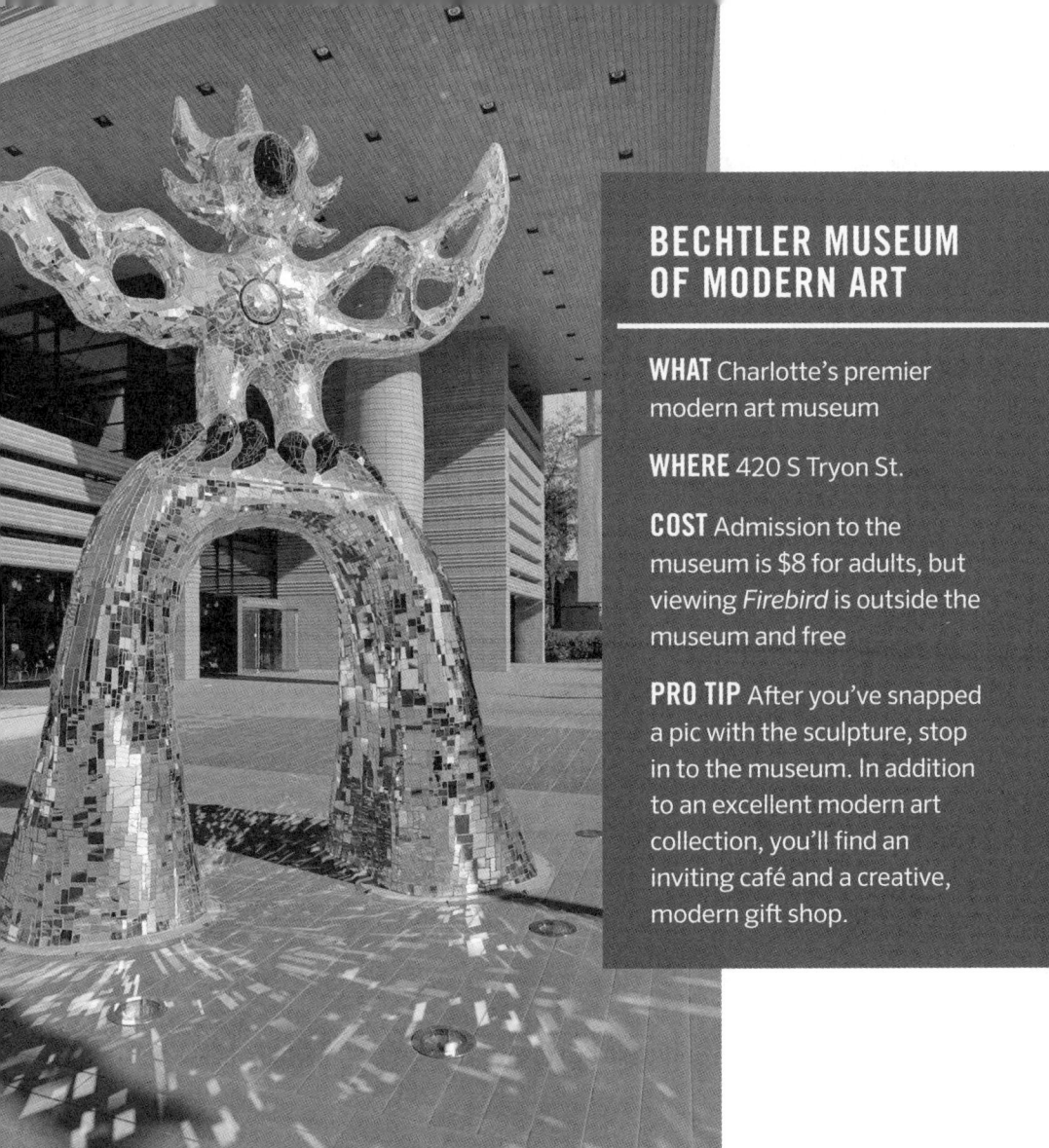

BECHTLER MUSEUM OF MODERN ART

WHAT Charlotte's premier modern art museum

WHERE 420 S Tryon St.

COST Admission to the museum is $8 for adults, but viewing *Firebird* is outside the museum and free

PRO TIP After you've snapped a pic with the sculpture, stop in to the museum. In addition to an excellent modern art collection, you'll find an inviting café and a creative, modern gift shop.

The playful Firebird sculpture in the plaza in front of Uptown's Bechtler Museum of Modern Art was crafted by French American artist Niki de Saint Phalle, and has become a favorite photography spot for locals and tourists alike.

Today, the bird is a fixture in Uptown, so much so that it even has a nickname to go with its mirrored-cover body and bell-bottom like legs: "The Disco Chicken."

32 BURIED TREASURE

Is Bank of America literally built on top of a gold mine?

It's well known that the Charlotte area was home to a gold rush in the early 1800s. It's why we have things like the Gold Rush Trolley system. But most of the mines are located outside of the city's center.

As it turns out, two of the largest mines, St. Catherine and Rudisill, actually had tunnels that ran beneath parts of Uptown—sometimes as far as four hundred feet down. Several shafts run parallel to South Mint St. and others are thought to run beneath Bank of America Stadium.

No one is certain of the locations of many of the tunnels, but when construction began on what is now Bank of America Corporate Center (it was then North Carolina National Bank) in the 1980s, workers discovered wooden frames of a mine still intact, along with an even more exciting discovery: flecks of gold in the rocks.

While gold mining has long since ended in Charlotte, an Australian-headquartered mining company is starting to mine gold again in nearby South Carolina. And the project is set to be the largest gold mining operation in the eastern United States.

Bank of America's corporate center is the tallest building in town and is attached to Founders Hall, with its picturesque atrium where you'll find the bank's heritage center.

BANK OF AMERICA HERITAGE CENTER

WHAT A museum where you can learn more about the city's long history in currency—in a location above former gold mines

WHERE In Founders Hall at the Bank of America Corporate Center

COST Free

PRO TIP The Heritage Center is owned by Bank of America and functions as a promotional component of the bank—it's attached to a store selling bank paraphernalia. However, Charlotte's banking industry has long been a large part of its history, and the center offers valuable insight into this legacy.

33 FAITH ON THE FARM

Why is there a barn with a giant cross on the front just a few miles outside of Uptown?

One of Charlotte's most famous former residents is evangelist Billy Graham. Before Graham was an internationally renowned Christian leader, he grew up on a local dairy farm. When the Billy Graham Library was being designed, the designers chose to pay homage to his bucolic background by housing the museum in a building shaped like an oversized barn, complete with a silo. The cross at its entrance is, of course, in reference to his Christian faith.

Inside, the forty-thousand-square-foot

Charlotte's Billy Graham Library is a favorite destination for visitors throughout the year, but is especially popular during the Christmas season. The holiday at the library includes a live nativity, horse-drawn carriage rides, story time for children, and Christmas dinner.

At the Billy Graham Library guests can tour exhibits of the famed evangelist's life and travels, dine at its Dairy Bar, and shop in its bookstore—all inside this giant barn-shaped building with a cross on its front.

BILLY GRAHAM LIBRARY

WHAT Library and museum dedicated to the renowned religious leader

WHERE 4330 Westmont Dr.

COST Free

PRO TIP The Memorial Prayer Garden is designed to be a peaceful site, and is home to the graves of Graham's wife, Ruth Bell Graham, and two close friends of the evangelist.

complex is much more sophisticated than its pastoral façade might lead one to believe. It features a "Journey of Faith" tour complete with multimedia presentations and memorabilia documenting Graham's years as a prestigious leader.

Visitors will also find Graham's childhood home, a bookstore and dairy bar cafe, a prayer garden, and the Billy Graham Evangelistic Association on the grounds. The facility's most whimsical nod to Graham's past—and a favorite for many of its younger visitors—is the mechanical "talking" cow that greets guests to the barn.

34. ITALIAN STYLE

Why is there a Tuscan Villa in the middle of Myers Park?

At first glance, you might assume that the Providence Road building known as The Villa is a recent addition, designed by an architect to mimic the popular Tuscan style. After all, the space is now filled with trendy shops and restaurants. But take a closer look. The tile-roofed and stucco-walled villa was built in the 1920s, and its owner was known to be just as dramatic and creative as her home.

Blanche Reynolds was a petite, red-haired, wealthy widow when she purchased the land for the home, but then on a trip to Italy in 1925 she met a Russian named Alexis Gourmajenko. The two married and moved into the home in 1926. Known for her love of the arts and travel, Blanche hired renowned New York City architect William L. Bottomley to design the villa. It ultimately featured eccentric luxuries like a leather-walled séance room, frescoes on the bedroom ceiling, and Charlotte's first swimming pool.

While today this former Providence Road mansion is known as The Villa, it's actually the Reynolds-Gourmajenko House, which has been designated as a historic site by Mecklenburg County.

Today, this Tuscan-style villa is home to luxury shops and upscale restaurants, like Stagioni. But it was originally built as an extravagant residence.

Blanche was known for her opulent parties—and for driving a Daimler around town with her two Dalmations in the backseat. Today, guests to The Villa's Stagioni restaurant can get a glimpse of her world in a black-and-white photo of the lavish celebration of her son's wedding in 1954, which is showcased in the restaurant.

STAGIONI

WHAT A restaurant in The Villa that best represents its former glory

WHERE 715 Providence Rd.

COST This is an upscale restaurant with entrees starting around $20

PRO TIP For the full Villa dining experience, stop in for a cocktail first at RuRu's Taco & Tequila, which is located behind the former home.

35 TALES FROM THE DUNHILL

Why are there claims that this popular Uptown hotel is haunted?

Today, The Dunhill is known as Charlotte's most historic hotel. But when the ten-story elegant landmark was built in 1929, it was one of several high-end Uptown hotels. It opened as The Mayfair Manor, featuring more than one hundred rooms, private bathrooms, and a luxurious penthouse.

But the hotel almost immediately developed a dark reputation. There are rumors that because it was one of the city's tallest buildings, several suicides occurred there during the Great Depression as people threw themselves from the top floors. Then, just twenty years after its opening, it was sold, renamed the James Lee Motor Inn, and slowly began to fall into disrepair.

Sometime around 1981, the building was abandoned until Dunhill Hotel Associates purchased it in 1987. At that point they began remodeling construction, essentially gutting the building to create the luxurious old world hotel that exists there today. As construction began though, there was an unexpected discovery: A human skeleton was found in an elevator shaft.

It's rumored that the Dunhill Hotel's room #906 is its most haunted, with stories of finger tapping on the night stand, dramatic changes in room temperature, and electronics turning on and off on their own.

From its penthouse complete with a working fireplace and stone balconies, to its swanky bar and charming lobby, Uptown's Dunhill Hotel offers hints of its history.

THE DUNHILL HOTEL

WHAT A historic and sophisticated hotel in Uptown Charlotte

WHERE 237 N Tryon St.

COST Room prices vary

PRO TIP No need to spend an evening in one of the rooms: Get a taste of The Dunhill's 1920s charm with a classic cocktail from its inviting lobby bar.

These ominous stories have led to claims of ghost sightings in the hotel. From strange smells to the sounds of tapping fingers, the stories vary. And while there's no definitive proof of any paranormal activity, it's certainly a hotel with its fair share of stories.

36 LOVE LOCKS

What's with all the padlocks on the patio fence at Amelie's French Bakery?

If you have ever traveled to the Pont des Arts, a bridge in Paris famous for being covered with "love locks" (before they were removed in 2015), then you know about the tradition. On the bridge, sweethearts attach padlocks to its railing, symbolizing their love. Usually their initials are inscribed on the lock before they toss its key into the Seine River below, symbolizing their unbreakable love.

Amelie's French Bakery may be Charlotte's closest approximation of Paris. Close your eyes as you take a bite of one of its croissants or macarons and you can almost imagine you're sitting in a sunny café with a view of the Eiffel Tower. Spend some time in its quirky interior filled with colorful décor and you can pretend you're on the Left Bank.

It's only natural then that Amelie's original location in NoDa (the popular neighborhood named for its central street, North Davidson) adopted the love lock tradition. And while there's no river to toss your key into afterwars, you can include your initials and then celebrate your love with another one of those macarons.

Amelie's French Bakery's patio fence of love locks is significantly smaller than the Parisian version, but its colorful locks still feature their own personality with signatures and words inscribed on many of the locks.

The next time you're stopping into the original location of Amelie's French Bakery, pause by its patio to notice all of the love locks attached to its fence.

AMELIE'S FRENCH BAKERY

WHAT An authentic French bakery known for its sweet pastries, creative décor, and late hours

WHERE 2424 N Davidson St.

COST Expect typical coffee shop prices

PRO TIP Want to really ensure unbreakable love? Buy your sweetheart one of the bakery's famed salted caramel brownies.

37 FLOWER POWER

Why is there a sign for a floral shop in Uptown with no actual shop?

In 1917 Louis G. Ratcliffe opened Ratfcliffe's Flowers at Latta Arcade in Uptown. Then, in 1929 the floral shop moved to the striking Mediterranean Revival building that is now Bernadin's restaurant on South Tryon. The Ratcliffes had long been in the flower business, and the family hung a neon green and white sign advertising their flowers just outside the shop.

During the 1950s, businesses on Tryon began removing their neon signs after it was decided that the streets appeared too cluttered. But Louis Ratcliffe, Jr., who was helping his father with the shop at the time, refused. Ratcliffe, a veteran who had fought in the Battle of the Bulge before returning to join the family business, didn't appreciate the city's government telling him what to do. And so the sign stayed.

The family flower shop stuck around until the late 1980s when the spot turned into a restaurant. Today, the two-story building which is known for its ornate details like cast

---

When Louis G. Ratcliffe originally opened his popular floral shop in 1917, it was adjacent to the Latta Arcade. During the 1920s, the business was booming and so he moved across the street and one block down into the unique space that is now Bernadin's restaurant.

While the floral shop itself is gone—and even its building as been moved up the block—the retro sign for Ratcliffe's Flowers still stands as a testament to a time when Charlotte's streets were filled with similar signs.

BERNADIN'S CHARLOTTE

WHAT A fine dining restaurant housed in Uptown's former historic Ratcliffe's Flowers shop

WHERE 2424 N Davidson St.

COST Dinner entrees start around $25

PRO TIP Look for the original Tiffany stained glass, stone floors, and impressive woodwork inside the restaurant. The building has housed several different restaurants since it was the floral shop. Bernadin's worked to preserve and promote many of the original details of the building.

iron railings and stained glass windows, still stands. (It was temporarily moved across Tryon Street in 2000 in order to build a parking garage beneath, and then moved seventy-five feet to the north of its original location.)

And just a few feet down the street in the adjacent Green, where the original building once stood, hangs the original historic Ratcliffe's neon sign, having come a long way from something city officials felt was cluttering the street.

38. NEWS FROM THE NORTH

Why is there a plaque in front of a seafood restaurant chain describing where the president of the Confederacy was standing on April 18, 1865?

President Abraham Lincoln was assassinated on the night of April 14, 1865 and pronounced dead on April 15. Not long before that, Jefferson Davis, who had been the president of the Confederacy during the Civil War, had fled his home in Richmond, Virginia.

The accounts of what happened vary, but this seems to be the general story: The former president and his cabinet were on the move, still having supporters in the South, of course, but fearing Union troops. In Charlotte, they were given a place to stay by a man from Massachusetts named Lewis F. Bates, who lived on South Tryon Street in the center of town. Davis was speaking to a group at the house when a telegram arrived for him, notifying him—and subsequently the crowd—that President Lincoln had been assassinated.

And this is where the history gets a little murky. The telegram gave the incorrect date of the assassination as

---

After hearing of Lincoln's death, Jefferson continued to flee, heading first for South Carolina and then Georgia before being captured in Irwinville, Ga. He was taken prisoner, but was ultimately released and never brought to trial. The charges for treason were dropped in 1867, and he moved to Mississippi, where he lived until his death in 1889.

It's easy to walk right over this plaque in the sidewalk just outside of McCormick & Schmick's in Uptown Charlotte. But it marks a spot that was once the steps of a home where the former president of the Confederacy heard the news of Lincoln's demise.

CHARLOTTE WALKING TOUR

WHAT A self-guided tour of Charlotte history

WHERE Center City Charlotte

COST Free

PRO TIP Visit CharlottesGotAlot.com/charlotte-walking-tour to take a self-guided walking tour around Uptown's historic, architectural, and artistic sites, where you're likely to see many landmarks like this one.

being April 11. And there are widely varying stories of Davis' reaction to the news. Regardless of those details, today a brass plaque commemorates the spot where the telegram was read. It's easy to miss on the busy sidewalk in front of McCormick & Schmick's in the middle of Uptown, but it's worth looking out for the next time you're walking by.

39 SPINNING WHEEL

What's the giant bronze wheel in the middle of Uptown?

From Chicago to Milan, there are six *Il Grande Disco* sculptures by Italian sculptor Arnaldo Pomodoro around the world. Charlotte's was installed in 1974 at what is now Bank of America Plaza at the corner of Trade and Tryon Streets to commemorate Mecklenburg's Declaration of Independence (see page 102) from England.

Originally, the six-ton, fifteen-foot disc turned on its axis, and passersby would push on it to watch the bronze wheel with its etched designs slowly spin. But at some point it became unable to turn and now is anchored in its spot.

For twenty-five years this was known as Charlotte's most iconic piece of public art, until the installation of Niki de Saint Phalle's *Firebird* in front of the Bechtler Museum of Modern Art. Oddly enough, the sculpture is often called the "Disco Wheel" based on its name and shape, while the *Firebird* is called the "Disco Chicken" based on its sparkle and poultry characteristics.

BANK OF AMERICA PLAZA

WHAT The forty-story Bank of America skyscraper and its adjacent outdoor area in the center of Uptown Charlotte

WHERE Corner of East Trade and South Tryon Streets

COST Free

PRO TIP In addition to *Il Grande Disco*, from the plaza you can see the four sculptures on the square representing commerce, industry, transportation, and future.

This large bronze wheel is a piece of art in the center of town. When it was first installed, the wheel spun, but today it stands still.

One of Charlotte's oldest pieces of public art, this piece features a plaque dated October 2, 1974, that begins with the words: "Our life today is one of crisis . . . of movement . . . of tension." This feels especially appropriate for a piece that once moved, but has been stationary for several decades.

40 HISTORIC HOTDOGS

What's the Uptown building with a happy looking hot dog painted on the side?

If you've driven or walked around Uptown, you've likely noticed the small brick building with a friendly looking hot dog painted on its exterior. It doesn't exactly blend in among the shiny skyscrapers—and that may be because it was there long before most of them.

Green's Lunch has been serving up hot dogs since 1926, when its original owner, Robert Green, opened the business offering hot dogs and hamburgers. It's seen famed faces from NFL star Cam Newton to renowned evangelist Billy Graham, but its menu hasn't changed much over the years. And neither has the price point. While you won't be paying 1920s prices, you'll still be getting one of Uptown's cheapest breakfasts or lunches at this casual spot.

GREEN'S LUNCH

WHAT A small, historic restaurant where you can order casual food at the counter

WHERE 309 W 4th St.

COST Prices are seriously low here, with hot dogs starting at $1.95 and hamburgers at $3

PRO TIP It's called Green's Lunch, but its breakfast is equally appealing. Try the local favorite: an omelette made with livermush.

Green's Lunch in Uptown Charlotte has been a local favorite for almost a century. And once you've tasted one of its hot dogs you'll understand why.

Diners order at the counter at Green's Lunch and then check out at the cashier once they have their food. It's fast-casual with a 1960's vibe. Once you've got your food and paid, slide into one of the booths and enjoy one of the city's best hotdogs.

41 BY THE LETTER

Why is there a museum dedicated to the alphabet in Waxhaw?

The charming town of Waxhaw, just south of Charlotte, is full of surprises. Historically, its claim to fame is being the birthplace of President Andrew Jackson and the home of the Waxhaw Indians—a somewhat odd mix of history, considering Jackson is widely known for the tragic Trail of Tears.

And while there is a museum in the town that is focused on the region's history, Waxhaw's most unexpected museum may be its Museum of the Alphabet. The small, brick structure just outside downtown is entirely focused on the history of alphabets.

William Cameron Townsend opened the museum in 1990. Townsend became interested in linguistics when he learned as a South American missionary that many people are unable to read the Bible in their language because a translation doesn't exist—and often the language doesn't even have an alphabet. He founded Wycliffe Bible Translators, the Summer

---

The Museum of the Alphabet features exciting exhibits like a 150-year-old Torah scroll. But JAARS' most unusual exhibit is inside the Mexico-Cardenas Museum. Cardenas gave the organization's leader Cameron Townsend a Chevrolet in 1938. Today, you'll find it parked inside the museum.

Sure, it doesn't look like much from the outside. And the concept of a museum dedicated to the alphabet may not sound exciting. But this small Waxhaw museum offers unique insight into the world's languages.

MUSEUM OF THE ALPHABET

WHAT A small museum in Waxhaw dedicated to the history of alphabets

WHERE It's part of the large JAARS headquarters at 6409 Davis Rd., Waxhaw

COST Free

PRO TIP Explore more than the alphabet. JAARS offers tours of its headquarters, where more than 600 people from around the world work on providing appropriate translated versions of the Bible. Then make a stop in the headquarters' Mexico-Cardenas Museum dedicated to Lazaro Cardenas, Mexico's president from 1934 to 1940, and a close friend of JAARS' founder, William Cameron Townsend.

Institute of Linguistics, and the Jungle Aviation and Radio Service (JAARS), all to help this cause.

Townsend was passionate about teaching others the historical importance of written words and their development, especially in relation to translations of the Bible, which is why he opened the small museum at JAARS headquarters in Waxhaw. The museum, which is broken into sections such as Hebrew or Cyrillic, features photographs, sculptures, and multimedia exhibits. Guests can take guided tours (if arranged in advance) or explore on their own.

42 LOST LAKE

Why did trolleys once run to an area in west Charlotte that's now just power lines and woods?

Between 1910 and 1933, Charlotte was home to a vibrant amusement park known for its beautiful lake, tall Ferris wheel, oversized carousel, petting zoo filled with exotic animals, roller coaster, casino, bowling alley, and a dance hall famed for its evenings of dancing (including a marathon dance contest that actually broke state records for longest time on the dance floor).

Lakewood Park was built by Edward Dilworth Latta, who had already developed the city's first streetcar suburb of Dilworth. He'd built Latta Park in that neighborhood, offering some of the same amusements. However, because he ran out of land there, he dismantled Latta Park and built Lakewood Park to the northwest of town. Latta had also been instrumental in developing the city's trolley line, and so he chose the location of the new park because he could run cars on railroad tracks already in place there.

Initially, the park thrived. For twenty years local families would ride the trolley, which ran through the center of

---

Online and in local archives you'll find a variety of images depicting scenes at Lakewood Park. In them you can see white string lights around the water's edge, colorful flower gardens filled with paths, a green-roofed lakeside pavilion with an American flag flying high overhead, and exotic animals in its petting zoo.

A drive around the Lakewood neighborhood today only offers hints of its amusement park past. Streets have names like Fairgrounds Avenue and Parkside Drive, and trolley lines seemingly lead to nowhere, but otherwise there's no sign of the former popular park.

LAKEWOOD NEIGHBORHOOD

WHAT The area of town where the famed amusement park once existed

WHERE To the west of town, where streets have names like Lakeview and Parkside, despite there being no lake or park today

COST Free

PRO TIP Railroad tracks still run where the trolley once did, giving a good idea of where the park and lake existed. And today the city continues to consider a greenway that would lead to this area, perhaps once again making it a destination for Charlotteans seeking relaxation just outside of the city.

the park, to go swimming and boating, dancing in its pavilion, picnicking by the lake, and viewing the live shows. It was advertised as a healthy place for fresh air and artesian well water.

Then the Great Depression hit and families no longer had the money for an excursion to the amusement park. People stopped visiting the park, and in 1936 a storm washed away the dam. The park was eventually torn down and the lake was filled in. Today, a power station and trees are all that stand in place of what was once known as Charlotte's Coney Island.

43 INTERIOR PLANS

Why is Uptown Charlotte connected by a series of interior walkways and tunnels?

In 1966 Charlotte leaders created the Charlotte Masterplan, often called the Odell Plan, after architect A.G. Odell. It had plans for a stadium, a zoo, skyscrapers, museums, and many other urban developments. Today, much of Charlotte's Uptown can be attributed to this plan, including its Overstreet Mall, a network of shops and restaurants connected through the interior of buildings and skywalks.

When the plan was being implemented, there were two major differences from modern day that affected the way the planners thought about street level retail. First, there were safety concerns in Uptown Charlotte that made pedestrians hesitant to be on the streets. The hope was that an interior mall and access between buildings would help with that fear.

But the biggest difference was the response to the automobile. At the time, it seemed that cars were a wonderful new invention that would change our movements

---

While Overstreet Mall does have some historic aspects, it's also fully in use today. You'll find spots like its Chick-fil-A to be especially full at lunch time and its shops, while they have no street frontage, are successful simply because of the foot traffic within the Uptown buildings.

Because of Overstreet Mall's series of hallways, enclosed pedestrian bridges, and walkways, Uptown can feel like a series of secret tunnels.

OVERSTREET MALL

WHAT A network of walkways connecting high-rises, shops, and restaurants in Uptown Charlotte

WHERE Primarily along Tryon St.

COST Free

PRO TIP Make sure to walk through the tunnel between Three Wells Fargo Center and Two Wells Fargo Center. It seems like an otherwise normal tunnel with carpeted floors, but its walls feature a bright rainbow of colors reaching from one end to the next.

entirely. People would no longer walk on the streets because they would drive everywhere. It didn't seem necessary to put retail stores or restaurants on street fronts or to keep them within walking distance of each other. So when Overstreet Mall was completed in the 1970s, it was with the idea of keeping the pedestrians inside, shopping and eating in the midlevel network of halls and atriums.

Today, for those who aren't familiar with it, Overstreet Mall can be somewhat confusing to navigate, and its crowds—especially at lunch hour—can be daunting. There are unmarked walkways and signs to follow arrows in parking garages as the Mall weaves from one side of town to the other. But on cold and rainy days or in the Southern summer heat, you can almost believe that those city planners were on to something.

44 SET UP CAMP

Why did the population of Charlotte almost double in 1917?

Until 1917, Charlotte had been a fairly quiet town, full of farmers and mill workers. Then, during World War I, the United States Army established Camp Greene on a farm just southwest of the city—and brought in forty thousand recruits to train at its facility. Quite suddenly, Charlotte, which had thirty-four thousand people according to the 1910 census, had doubled in size.

At six thousand acres, it was a massive camp going from downtown Charlotte all the way to the Catawba River and even into Gaston County. There, soldiers learned military drills and dug trenches, simulating the war happening in Europe and training for combat. The camp also included a hospital, a post office, and an airfield.

Ultimately, more than sixty thousand soldiers lived on the base—and Charlotte welcomed them with enthusiasm. But as soon as the war ended, Camp Greene's soldiers

---

In the Camp Greene neighborhood, which was formerly part of the military facility, you'll find Camp Greene Park. Take a walk in the park's woods and you'll find concrete foundations that were left behind after World War I was over, the facility had closed, and the men had left.

Just off the busy Wilkinson Boulevard west of town you'll find the quiet Camp Greene neighborhood, which includes the historic Dowd House. The home served as the headquarters of the Camp Greene army camp during WWI.

HISTORIC DOWD HOUSE

WHAT A farmhouse built in 1879 that was the headquarters of Camp Greene

WHERE 2216 Monument St.

COST Free

PRO TIP The home, which is a designated historic site, is open on the third day of each month and visits must be scheduled by reservation (704-398-2260). Originally the center of a 250-acre farm and once owned by the publisher of *The Charlotte News*, the house's history goes beyond Camp Greene.

began to leave and eventually the entire camp was shut down. Today the Dowd family farmhouse, which was used as the camp headquarters, is all that remains. But many believe that this camp forever changed Charlotte as it brought outside attention to the once quiet town.

BANK OF AMERICA (page 6)

AMELIE'S FRENCH BAKERY (page 72)

DOWD HOUSE (page 88)

ASIAN LIBRARY IN MIDTOWN (page 108)

DUKE MANSION IN MYERS PARK (page 112)

QUEENS ROAD IN MYERS PARK (page 144)

TROLLEY WALK (page 182)

LAKE NORMAN (page 206)

UPTOWN RITZ-CARLTON (page 192)

NODA'S NEIGHBORHOOD THEATRE (page 150)

THE VILLA (page 68)

FREEDOM PARK (page 188)

BILLY GRAHAM LIBRARY (page 66)

45 FAR EASTERN EXPOSURE

Why does Charlotte have a library with almost one hundred fifty thousand Asian books?

You've likely seen the Asian Library in Midtown, just across from the Metropolitan shopping area, but most Charlotteans haven't actually ventured inside. After all, Charlotte's population is only five percent Asian and the thousands of books inside this library are primarily written in Chinese, Japanese, Korean, and Vietnamese.

Opened in 1985, today this is the largest private Asian library in the United States. It's the home of *The Asian Herald* newspaper whose publisher, Ki-Hyun Chun, launched the library from his private collection. In addition to featuring an incredible selection of books ranging from children's literature to self-help, the library often offers language learning and various other classes.

Ki-Hyun Chun's resume in Charlotte goes far beyond founding this library and the Asian Herald. Born in Seoul, South Korea, Chun helped organize the first Asian church in Charlotte, opened the city's Asian Language Institute, and established the Asia Pacific Caucus in North Carolina. He serves on many local boards and has received seemingly countless awards for his work.

While this building off Kings Drive may not look like a traditional library on the outside, inside you'll find thousands of books in Asian languages and about Asia, all in an elegant library setting.

THE ASIAN LIBRARY

WHAT A private library featuring books in Asian languages

WHERE 1339 Baxter St.

COST Membership is $10

PRO TIP If you can't read Asian languages, but are interested in Asia, you're in luck. The library features almost 10,000 books written in English about Asian cultures and history.

It's worth stopping in just to see this culturally rich spot. Tiled floors and replicas of statues like Rodin's *The Thinker* set the scene for learning in the two-story space. And if you find a book that intrigues you, membership is open to anyone and is only ten dollars.

46 LOCAL DELICACY

What is livermush and where did it come from?

If you're dining at one of Charlotte's more casual restaurants—especially those that have been around awhile and serve breakfast—you might notice this distinctly unappetizing sounding dish on the menu. And unfortunately, while the dish is tasty, the name is a fairly apt description.

The dish is made by mixing (and mushing) a combination of pig liver, headparts, and cornmeal, and then forming the mixture into a loaf. Generally, livermush is served in slices that have been cut from the loaf and then fried until golden brown. Often served simply on sandwiches or biscuits, it's a local favorite. The town of Shelby, to the west of Charlotte, even hosts an annual Livermush Festival dedicated to the dish.

There are different theories as to the origins of the dish. Some say that it evolved during the Civil War, when the inhabitants of western North Carolina were desperate for food and didn't want to waste any parts of the hog. Others

---

One of the more unusual livermush offerings is a livermush sushi roll served at Shelby restaurant Sushi Dojo. The roll, aptly named "Hee Haw Roll," features livermush, cream cheese, and crab. It's rolled and then deep-fried, making it an unusual mix of Japanese and Southern fare.

Livermush didn't get lucky with its name. But locals love this pork dish, which is often served fried and on bread.

MUSH, MUSIC, AND MUTTS

WHAT The annual festival in Shelby, NC, which produces much of the region's livermush.

WHERE Shelby's downtown court square

COST Free

PRO TIP In addition to its livermush offerings, the festival also highlights the region's local breweries and musicians. If you can't make it to the festival, stop in to the Shelby Café, a local diner that has been serving the popular dish for decades.

say that it came from German settlers who came to the Appalachian mountains via Pennsylvania, where a similar dish, scrapple, is served.

Regardless of its history, Charlotte has adopted the dish as its own, and today you'll find it in grocery stores, gas stations, and even in upscale restaurants.

47 PRESIDENTIAL APPEAL

What home was once visited by an actual U.S. President and portrayed the home of a vice-president on a hit television series?

The Duke Mansion in the Myers Park neighborhood of Charlotte has a storied and celebrity-studded past. It was built in 1915 and then tripled in size in 1919 when James B. Duke (as in Duke University and Duke Energy) purchased the home.

In 1929, the Cannon family, who made their money in textiles, became the owners of the home and hosted their daughter Frances's wedding on its grounds. Frances had dated a Harvard University student named John F. Kennedy for a year, but her family had discouraged their relationship and it eventually ended. However, there were no hard feelings and when she married a man named John Hersey, Kennedy attended her wedding.

The home went through various other owners—even at one point being split into condominiums—before becoming a historic inn and meeting center known as The Mansion. Today, it's been restored to its former

---

To celebrate its 100th anniversary in 2015, the Duke Mansion revamped and expanded its gardens—and opened them to the public. Today, passersby can step onto the 4.5-acre property and wander down its beautifully manicured paths.

The historic Duke Mansion, which is tucked into the Myers Park neighborhood, features twenty guest rooms, a guest library, and four and a half acres of gardens.

glory and when the Emmy-winning TV series *Homeland* was filming in Charlotte in 2013, it served as the set for fictional Vice President William Walden's home.

THE DUKE MANSION

WHAT A former private historic mansion turned elegant inn

WHERE 400 Hermitage Rd.

COST Visitors can visit the mansion's gardens for free, or book a stay at the inn for which prices vary

PRO TIP If you'd rather not stay the full night, but want to experience The Mansion's full splendor, make reservations for a Picnic in the Garden. The site's chef prepares a picnic basket and a bottle of wine, and a blanket is set out in the gardens for an evening dinner. The cost is $75.

48 FLIGHT SHOW

Where can you get up close and personal with an eagle?

Carolina Raptor Center isn't your average museum. The fifty-seven-acre facility is both a preserve and a hospital of sorts for its collection of hunter avians. And while you'll find all the usual aspects of a museum, including educational exhibits and even a gift shop, its live raptors are its most unusual attraction.

The Raptor Trail, which is a little less than a mile long, features more than thirty species of raptors and birds of prey. You're likely to catch a glimpse of a pair of nesting bald eagles or a spectacled owl, along with a variety of hawks and vultures.

For the ultimate behind-the-scenes look at the birds, check out the raptor hospital. It was originally built in the basement of the biology building at nearby UNC–Charlotte in 1981 before moving to the Center. Today, it's the largest raptor rehabilitation facility in the United States.

CAROLINA RAPTOR CENTER

WHAT A living museum and animal hospital dedicated to showcasing and rehabilitating raptors

WHERE 6000 Sample Rd., Huntersville

COST $10 for adults

PRO TIP The best time to visit may be during the summer season when the Center offers the Talons Summer Flight Show featuring trainers putting birds through their paces on free flight as guests watch from the amphitheater.

Carolina Raptor Center features a variety of birds of prey including owls, hawks, and eagles—and the chance to get up close with all of them on your visit.

To get "nose-to-beak" with one of the birds, sign up for one of the Raptor Encounters, where participants can be up-close with eagles, owls, and vultures—and even have their photos taken with the birds.

Carolina Raptor Center has two bald eagles they've named Derek and Savannah who nest in the center's aviary each year. In 2006, the pair hatched and released two chicks, which were the first hatched in captivity in the state. Since then, four additional chicks have been hatched in the aviary.

49 SIGN OF THE TIMES

Why is there a vintage rotating sign with a penguin on it in Plaza Midwood?

On the corner of Commonwealth and Thomas Avenues is Comida, a chic, modern Mexican restaurant featuring cocktails and small plates. From the corner you can see the patio of the always-busy Common Market, a trendy yoga studio, and a new craft brewery. And on that same corner sits the Penguin Drive-In sign with an illustration of a penguin, harkening to decades past.

The Penguin's history is a source of controversy for many long-time Charlotteans. The Drive-In first opened for business in 1954 in Plaza Midwood as a casual burger joint, and its owner, Jim Ballentine, ran it himself for decades. Then, in 2000 he turned it over to a group of managers who made it a favorite in the then-edgy neighborhood. It was famous for cold beers and hot fried pickles.

In 2010, Ballentine's daughter, Lisa, took it back over and pushed out the managers. The neighborhood, which had adopted the restaurant as its icon, rebelled, refusing

---

If you're feeling nostalgic for The Penguin, its old sign isn't the only way to reminisce. Queen City Gear offers a line of "Plaza Midwood: Home of the dead Penguin" items complete with an image of a fallen penguin. From pint glasses to t-shirts, you can own the memory of one of the neighborhood's most famed spots.

While the Penguin restaurant has long since closed its doors, the famed diner's sign still remains on its Plaza Midwood corner as a reminder of the neighborhood's rich past.

to patronize what had been a famous, always-full restaurant. And thus began its decline until it officially closed its doors in 2015.

Comida, which is in the space now, did extensive renovations and redesign on the restaurant's interior, making it almost unrecognizable for those who had frequented it as a burger joint in its past life. But, for now, Comida's owner has left the sign on the corner. Which, for longtime neighborhood restaurant-goers, feels right.

COMIDA

WHAT A sophisticated restaurant serving Mexican fare in the former Penguin Drive-In location

WHERE 1205 Thomas Ave. in the Plaza Midwood neighborhood

COST Food and drink prices vary

PRO TIP The restaurant was extensively renovated inside, but its 1950s-style exterior is much the same. And touches that remain from the original building can be seen on the interior as well, such as the glass block windows.

50 WHAT A DRAG

Where can you find an abandoned strip of track where cars used to race at more than 100 mph?

Charlotte has a long history with racing. As home to the NASCAR Hall of Fame and one of the country's most impressive tracks, it is undeniably a city that likes fast cars. One of the earlier spots where locals raced their own souped-up vehicles was a place called Shuffletown Dragway. Local residents, who preferred that the dangerous racing not happen on their public roads, originally built the track from dirt before paving it in 1964.

The races, which included cars and motorcycles, would draw crowds of thousands. But as Charlotte grew and the area developed, local homeowners grew tired of the noise, and in 1991, the track officially closed.

In 2010, the county developed the area as a park featuring baseball fields and a playground, but if you go past the fields and the dog park, you'll see a strip of pavement resembling an old street—and you can almost hear the roar of the cars that once raced there.

For those hoping to catch a glimpse of the Shuffletown Dragway's old glory days, you're in luck. Search for Shuffletown Dragway on YouTube and you'll find many videos featuring the loud and fast cars, excited announcers, and a track lined with spectators for the race.

Charlotte—home of the NASCAR Hall of Fame—has always loved its fast cars, so it should come as no surprise that there are still the remains of what was once a drag strip in Shuffletown Park just off I-485.

SHUFFLETOWN PARK

WHAT A public park that sits on the former location of the Shuffletown Dragway

WHERE 9500 Bellhaven Blvd.

COST Free

PRO TIP Stop in for a bite at the nearby Shuffletown Grill, a diner-style restaurant that has been around since 1957. It pays homage to the drag strip through photos and trophies around the restaurant—and you're likely to even find a person or two who likes to talk about the track's former glory.

119

51 MECK DEC

Was Charlotte the first colonial city to declare its independence from Great Britain?

On May 20, 1775, one year before the signing of the Declaration of Independence, leaders in Charlotte signed a resolution by the citizens of Mecklenburg County declaring that they had separated themselves from Great Britain. It was read aloud on the courthouse steps at the intersection of Trade and Tryon Streets, and ultimately Captain James Jack carried it by horseback to the Second Continental Congress in Philadelphia.

Unfortunately for Charlotte, at the time Congress was debating reconciliation with the King and so the declaration was generally ignored. There is even quite a bit of dispute over whether or not it ever actually existed, as the document wasn't published until 1819—forty years after it was supposedly written. (Thomas Jefferson famously disputed its existence, namely

---

One of the best ways to get a glimpse into Charlotte's history around this period is on the Charlotte Liberty Walk. You've likely seen the guiding pavers in uptown with their images of Captain Jack. There are fifteen sites along the walk, most of which are historical markers or plaques telling the story of what stood in that spot in the past.

Many claim that Charlotte was the first spot to declare independence from the British—and that Captain James Jack rode his horse to Philadelphia to share the region's news.

CAPTAIN JAMES JACK STATUE

WHAT The life-size bronze statue of Captain James Jack on horseback for his famous ride to Philadelphia to deliver the declaration

WHERE The corner of Fourth St. and Kings Dr.

COST Free

PRO TIP Look closely at the face. When the sculptor, Chas Fagan, was creating the statue, he used a local horse trainer and owner Bill Calvert as a model. And this wasn't the first time Calvert had portrayed Captain Jack. It's also Calvert's face you'll see on the packaging for the popular local craft beer, Olde Mecklenburg Brewery's Capt. Jack Pilsner.

because the language is so similar to the actual Declaration of Independence that he wrote, that it would appear he might have plagiarized.)

Nonetheless, Charlotte has embraced the lore of the declaration, even holding Meck Dec Day celebrations each year. In Charlotte, you'll find a statue of Captain James Jack on his way to deliver the declaration. More significantly, the North Carolina flag and seal feature the date of its alleged signing: May 20, 1775.

52 COVERT COLLECTION

Who are the people behind Charlotte's most famous public art?

In 1991, something happened that forever changed the arts scene in Charlotte. A small group of aesthetically inclined philanthropic donors established a fund they called the Queen's Table. It was meant to provide money—and lots of it—for projects that would enhance the quality of life in the city. Since then, inevitably, when new pieces of impressive public art are installed around town, they can be traced back to one place: Queen's Table.

The members of the group are anonymous, but their contributions to the city are far from it. In addition to some of Charlotte's most notable art, like the Sculptures on the Square at Trade and Tryon and Queen Charlotte at the Charlotte-Douglas International Airport, the private group has also funded the wind sculpture on West Trade Street and, most recently, *Ainsa III*, the steel sitting man on the UNC Charlotte Center City campus.

QUEEN CHARLOTTE STATUE

WHAT A fifteen-foot bronze statue of the Queen City's namesake by artist Ramond Kaskey

WHERE Charlotte-Douglas International Airport

COST Free

PRO TIP Until 1990, the statue had welcomed visitors from a highly visible location just outside the main building. But recent new construction at the airport forced a move for the 2.5-ton structure. She's temporarily between the two daily parking decks, but will likely be ultimately placed somewhere else on the property.

An anonymous group of called the Queen's Table has donated some of the city's most famous pieces of public art, like this Queen Charlotte statue at Charlotte Douglas International Airport.

So, look for their many contributions beautifying Charlotte, but don't expect to learn the names of the people who put them there. The generous members of Queen's Table remain one of the city's best-kept secrets.

While many of the dedications from the Queen's Table are more traditional works of sculpture, Ainsa III in the UNC Charlotte Center City plaza stands out from the crowd. The 12.5-foot-tall stainless steel piece features letters from nine different alphabets, which form the silhouette of a seated figure.

53 INTO THE WOODS

Why is there a tropical rainforest in the middle of Uptown Charlotte?

It's not often that you find a place deemed an urban rainforest, but that's exactly what you'll find inside Discovery Place museum in Uptown Charlotte. The science and technology museum first opened in 1981, but remains at the forefront of science innovation with its exhibits today. One of its most popular longtime exhibits is the authentic rainforest, growing right inside the building.

The rainforest is there to teach those who visit the museum about the importance of biodiversity. Inside it you'll find a forest floor full of frogs and turtles, lush trees, free-flying exotic birds, and tree-dwelling reptiles—including a ball python and several iguanas.

Possibly the most notable thing about this miniature rainforest is its balmy weather. Even on Charlotte's coldest winter day, the temperature inside this part of the museum is hot and humid, giving museum guests the impression they've stepped off North Tryon Street and into Central America.

DISCOVERY PLACE

WHAT A science and technology museum with several Charlotte locations

WHERE 301 N Tryon St.

COST Adult admission is $17, children are $13

PRO TIP Plan your visit around catching one of the films in the museum's IMAX Theatre. It's the largest IMAX Dome Theatre in the Carolinas, and it offers an up-close movie experience unlike anything else.

Inside Discovery Place museum in Uptown you'll find science exhibits, aquariums full of unusual creatures, and even a rainforest complete with plants, animals, and tropical temperatures.

One of the best times for grown-ups to visit this child-friendly museum is during its monthly Science on the Rocks nights. On those nights, the museum transforms to a strictly 21 and up venue featuring entertaining demos, special guests, and a drinks bar. Each night has a different theme (and guests often dress up), so check the website to find the best one for you.

54 THE BIBLICAL BENCH

Why is there a sculpture that appears to be Jesus on a Davidson bench?

When Davidson's St. Alban's Episcopal Church first installed a statue that depicts Jesus as a homeless man sleeping on a bench in 2014, there were some mixed feelings in the community. One woman even called the police, thinking she was reporting an actual homeless man sleeping on the church's property.

The bronze statue certainly gets your attention. At first glance, it appears to be simply a statue of a homeless man on a bench. But when you look closely, his uncovered feet are pierced with wounds from crucifixion. It's a powerful and provocative statement, and one that drew national attention to the small and affluent college town just north of Charlotte when it was first installed.

The statue was the first *Homeless Jesus* piece on display in the United States, but many more have been installed since—including one in Rome that was

JESUS THE HOMELESS STATUE

WHAT A sculpture depicting Jesus as a homeless man by Canadian sculptor Timothy Schmalz

WHERE 301 Caldwell Lane, Davidson, at St. Alban's Episcopal Church

COST Free

PRO TIP The artist's website describes the sculpture as being inspired by Matthew 25:40, which says, "Truly, I say to you, as you did it to one of the least of these my brothers, you did it to me."

This bench outside of St. Alban's Episcopal Church in Davidson often causes passersby to do a double take. The sculpture depicts Jesus as a homeless man sleeping on the bench.

presented to Pope Francis. And while the one in Davidson may have initially startled some viewers, there are those in the community who now often come to sit by its feet and pray.

When the *Homeless Jesus* statue was first installed, it was so lifelike that it frightened several local residents. Charlotte WCNC station reported that one woman even called the police saying that she was "concerned for the safety of the neighborhood."

55 TRANSPORTATION AUTHORITY

Did Bank of America's former CEO build the Charlotte Transit Center to avoid having to see buses outside his office?

No one can deny the power of former chief executive of Bank of America Hugh McColl—especially in Charlotte. McColl ran NationsBank for fifteen years before engineering the merger between it and Bank of America in 1998. He stepped down from the role in 2001, but continues to be a leader in the city many say he built.

From bringing teams like the Panthers and the Hornets to town, to financing construction throughout the area, McColl revitalized and changed the face of Charlotte. (And that's without mentioning his role in causing Charlotte to become the second-largest banking center in the country.)

But perhaps one of the most fascinating examples of his power was his choice to fund the building of Uptown's transit center in 1995. According to a 2005 *News & Observer* article, former Charlotte Mayor Richard Vinroot was once having a conversation with McColl at a cocktail party about

---

While the Charlotte Transportation Center opened for business in 1995, it would be 12 more years before the center also served as a station for the LYNX Blue Line light rail. Talks about building a light rail had begun in Charlotte as early as the mid-1980s, but official planning for the line didn't begin until 1999.

Today, Charlotte's Transportation Center, which opened in 1995, is a modern and well-oiled machine with buses and a light rail lining bringing passengers to and from the station.

CHARLOTTE TRANSPORTATION CENTER

WHAT The transit station in Uptown Charlotte, which serves both buses and the LYNX Blue Line

WHERE 310 E Trade St.

COST Free

PRO TIP As part of the Charlotte Area Transit System's "Arts in Transit" program, you'll find several pieces of art around the center. Look for the bronze drinking fountain basins that were designed by artist Nancy Blum to look like North Carolina's state flower, the dogwood.

the city's lack of bus shelters. Vinroot supported the idea of an Uptown transit center, but said that City Council had no interest in making it happen. According to the article, McColl asked, "What if I helped you build it?"

A 2004 document from the National Center of Transit research notes that in addition to concern about bus passengers not having a comfortable transfer location, there was also another issue: The dozens of buses making stops around town were causing congestion on Tryon Street—in front of McColl's office in NationsBank.

Regardless of why he did it, McColl was ultimately responsible for the Charlotte Transportation Center. NationsBank spent $10 million helping to create the modern transit center, which opened in 1995, and features restaurants, stores, and, of course, a Bank of America branch.

56 UNDER THE DOME

What local building broke records for having the largest unsupported steel dome in the world?

These days, it's easy to drive past Bojangles Coliseum on Independence Boulevard and barely notice the sixty-year-old structure. After all, in comparison to many of Charlotte's new and shiny arenas, it's small and appears dated. But this building may have one of the richest and most varied stories in the Queen City's past.

When it opened in 1955, the Coliseum—then known as the Charlotte Coliseum—was the largest unsupported steel dome in the world, at more than 332 feet wide and 112 feet high. It had almost ten thousand seats, but when Billy Graham gave the opening dedication address, almost 13,000 people crowded into the new and futuristic space.

Since then, the Coliseum has hosted an incredible variety of events. From symphonies to figure skaters, it's been one of the city's premier entertainment venues. Ringling Bros. Circus made its debut at the Coliseum in

---

In many ways the Charlotte Coliseum (now Bojangles Coliseum) put Charlotte on the map. Creating an arena of this scale during that period was considered innovative—and its over-sided dome attracted even more attention. The Coliseum was featured in numerous national news publications, and quickly became a draw for big acts.

Known now as Bojangles Coliseum, this structure off Indepence Boulevard to the east of town was built in 1955 as the Charlotte Coliseum. It's also been known as Indpendence Arena and Cricket Arena.

BOJANGLES COLISEUM

WHAT A two-hundred-thousand-square-foot entertainment venue built in 1955

WHERE 2700 E Independence Blvd.

COST Varies depending on event

PRO TIP The Coliseum has undergone extensive renovations in recent years to bring it up to modern standards, while still keeping its retro vibe. One of the easiest ways to get a glimpse inside is to attend a Charlotte Checkers home game. The local ice hockey team began playing in the Coliseum in 2015.

1957, and over the next fifty years, more than two hundred circus events drew crowds to the arena.

But it wasn't just for playful entertainment. Graham was only the first of many notable and important speakers who were guests of the Coliseum. President Richard Nixon, former first lady Jacqueline Kennedy, and David Letterman have been among those on the stage. And many of the most famous musical performers of the last half-century made a stop under this dome. From Elvis Presley, Ray Charles, The Rolling Stones, Bruce Springsteen, and Bob Dylan to John Legend and Alicia Keys, this Coliseum has seen it all.

57 INTRIGUING INTERSECTION

Why do Providence and Queens Roads both turn at their intersection?

Anyone who has ever arrived at this destination and doubted their GPS understands the bizarre intersection of these two roads. Rather than crossing the intersection to continue on the road you've been traveling on, you must sharply turn. The reason for this dates back to the early half of the twentieth century.

At that time, Myers Park, the neighborhood where these streets are located, included trolley tracks running down what is now the landscaped median on Queens Road. The plan was designed so that the trolley could make a large loop before going back into town. In 1912, the trolley's loop was named Queens Road after Queen Charlotte.

At that time, it was simple to understand. The trolley was on Queens Road and other streets like Providence Road would lead to the edge of the loop. Then, trolley

---

For a more tangible piece of history left behind by the Myers Park streetcar era, head just a few blocks down Queens Road to its intersection with Hermitage. There is a historic stone structure that was built in 1912 and once acted as a streetcar waiting station.

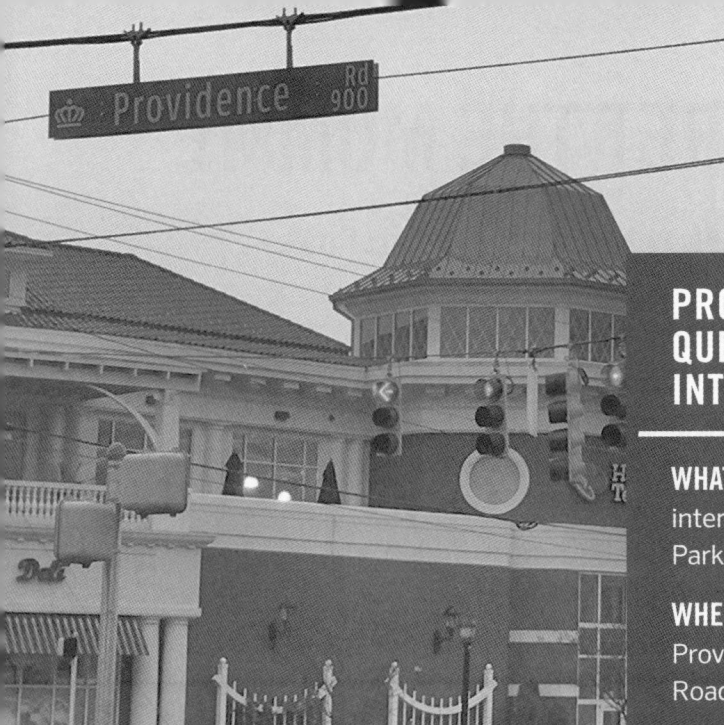

PROVIDENCE AND QUEENS ROAD INTERSECTION

WHAT The confusing intersection of two of Myers Park's most prominent roads

WHERE Intersection of Providence and Queens Roads

COST None

PRO TIP Each year, one of Charlotte's most notable fundraisers is held on the loop where the trolley once ran on Queens Road. 24 Hours of Booty, presented by the Levine Cancer Institute, features a 24-hour bike ride on the loop. Today, Charlotteans call this area "the booty loop" and it's a local favorite for runners and bikers throughout the year.

Things get confusing at the busy Myers Park intersection, where staying on either Queens or Providence Roads requires a turn.

service ended in 1938 and intersections became much more confusing. Today, the crossroads that don't actually cross may be Charlotte's most bizarre intersection—and always one that drives newcomers crazy.

133

58 MARGARET THE MUMMY

What's the real story behind North Carolina's only mummy?

The tale of North Carolina's only resident mummy is shrouded in mystery. Margaret the Mummy, who has been in an Iredell County museum just north of Charlotte, since 1957, has many stories associated with her provenance—and some of those stories are contradictory.

Inside her coffin, there are markings that indicate she lived around three thousand years ago during Egypt's 22nd Dynasty. Then, during the late 1800s, a Baptist missionary from Pennsylvania acquired her. (It seems likely the mummy was obtained from a tomb raider. The story goes that she was wrapped in an oriental carpet to be smuggled out.)

The missionary placed her in a museum just outside of Philadelphia, which is where her remains remained until

---

Margaret the Mummy actually has her own website (www.margaretthemummy.org) and can be followed on Facebook, Twitter, and Instagram for those who are particularly interested in the latest on the three-thousand-year-old mummy. And for younger historical scholars, there's an illustrated book for children called Margaret the Mummy: The Story That Was Never Told.

Margaret the Mummy is on display north of Charlotte in Statesville. As North Carolina's only mummy, she has a past shrouded in intrigue and mystery.

that museum closed in the 1950s. At that point, a paleontologist from Statesville acquired her for Iredell Museums, where she arrived via eighteen-wheeler wrapped in a blanket. And after her arrival, a contest among local schoolchildren secured her the name Margaret.

Today, with the exception of the occasional traveling exhibit, Margaret can be found in the museum. But her past is still a mystery waiting to be solved. It's possible that archived documents at Emory University tell the story of her voyage to America, and it's likely that archeologists and historians still have much to learn about mummies like Margaret. But for now, her story is best learned by paying her a visit just up the road.

IREDELL MUSEUMS

WHAT A museum in Statesville featuring art and artifacts from around the world

WHERE 134 Court St., Statesville

COST $6 per person

PRO TIP In addition to Margaret the Mummy, the museum also features works by Salvador Dali, Kenneth Noland, and Kathe Kolwitz, as well as pre-Columbian pottery.

59 SAVED BY THE BELL

Why does Heist Brewery ring a bell every Sunday at noon?

Every Sunday morning crowds flock in to NoDa neighborhood's Heist Brewery for its famed brunch buffet when the doors open at 10 a.m. Two hours later, the brewery rings a bell at its bar, and the sound is occasionally met by cheers from the crowd. The bell is the brewery's signal that it's 12 p.m. and therefore legal to begin serving drinks in the state of North Carolina.

Like many states, North Carolina has laws known as blue laws, which restrict some Sunday activities for religious reasons. Historically, the banned activities have

HEIST BREWERY

WHAT A restaurant and brewery in Charlotte's NoDa neighborhood

WHERE 2909 N Davidson St.

COST Menu prices vary

PRO TIP While you can't sample the brewery's beers before noon on Sunday, they're definitely worth a taste. And since Heist is open from 11 a.m. until 2 a.m. most days, there's plenty of time to enjoy its craft beer and bites on the other six days of the week.

Popular belief is that these laws were called blue laws because they were originally printed on blue paper. However, there's no real evidence to suggest this. It seems likely that the term came from 17th century slang, which called those following rigid and puritanical moral codes "blue."

Heist Brewery in the NoDa neighborhood is a local favorite for its small batch beers, craft cocktails, and large brunches.

included anything from furniture sales to recreational activities. Today, most of these laws have been repealed, but the sale of alcoholic beverages remains prohibited on Sunday mornings in some states.

In North Carolina, it's not legal to sell any kind of alcohol before noon on Sundays. Which means that as brunch has gained popularity in recent years, restaurants and drinking establishments like Heist have found playful ways to promote their drinks once they can legally serve them to customers.

And while you'll likely hear some grumbling from customers in the mood for a mimosa before the clock strikes twelve, this is far from the state or city's strangest law. The state's other blue law prohibits gun hunting between 9:30 a.m. and 12:30 p.m. on Sundays. And plenty of other laws, from the length of time a bingo game can last (five hours maximum) to what animals can plow cotton fields (not elephants), are still on the books.

60 OFF TRACK

What made Charlotte's trolley cars stop running?

Charlotte is undeniably proud of its historic trolley system—so much so, that the city recently installed the streetcar running from Uptown into Elizabeth, harkening to its glory days in the first half of the twentieth century.

While trolley cars were once a major form of local transportation, as well as the impetus for development of many of Charlotte's "streetcar suburbs" like Dilworth or Myers Park, the system virtually disappeared around the same time as World War II.

It's widely recognized that trollies across the country began to disappear with the advent of the automobile. With Ford Motor Co. making it possible for the average family to own a car, mass transportation began to seem like a thing of the past. In Charlotte, this was likely the case as well, but there was one other incident here that may have hurried the process of closing trolley operations.

In 1931, forty-eight passengers and one operator were on a trolley going through Uptown. Around 7:30 a.m., as the trolley approached the train tracks on West Trade Street, so did a southbound passenger train. The watchman, who

---

For a different view of the trolley's past, go to Atherton Market in South End. Now a popular farmers market, this building was once a "trolley barn," where the trolleys were stored at the Atherton Mill Station, which was the southern terminus for the line. You'll find the old tracks leading straight up to the trolley-sized door.

GOLD LINE STREETCAR

WHAT In 2015, Charlotte opened a streetcar line for the first time in seventy-seven years.

WHERE The cars run on tracks that stretch 1.5 miles from Elizabeth's Presbyterian Hospital to Uptown's Spectrum Center.

COST Free to ride

PRO TIP The streetcar arrives at six stations along the line approximately every fifteen minutes, and a one-way trip from start to finish is about ten minutes.

While it's been decades since trolley cars were a main part of Charlotte transportation, you can experience some of the cars' former glory on the new Gold Line Streetcar, which runs from Uptown into the Elizabeth neighborhood.

raised and lowered the gates, never saw the train approaching and allowed the trolley onto the tracks, where the train barreled into it.

The glass windows of the trolley shattered and passengers were thrown through them as it was hurled from the track. One passenger was thrown onto the track, where the train rolled over him and severed his foot. While miraculously there were no fatalities, of the forty-nine on board, forty-three were injured. It would be seven years before the trolley system officially ceased operations in Charlotte, but for many, the 1931 accident marked the beginning of the end of the once-popular mode of transportation.

61 SARTORIAL STATUE

Why is the statue at the corner of Providence and Queens Roads constantly being dressed up and decorated?

For Charlotte's many newcomers, the sculpture of a man at the busy intersection of Providence and Queens Roads may simply seem like an unusual mascot, often decorated with scarves or signs to wish someone happy birthday or congratulations. But for longtime Charlotteans, its origins are nostalgic.

The statue features the late Myers Park resident, Hugh McManaway. Born in 1912, McManaway was labeled as mentally handicapped. He had many talents though, not the least of which was making friends around the community. At some point in the 1950s, McManaway became the neighborhood's self-appointed traffic director, waving on traffic with a white towel at the notoriously confusing intersection.

After his mother died in 1963, McManaway lived alone in his family's Myers Park mansion, but remained a

---

While the beloved traffic director Hugh McManaway was labeled as metally handicapped, there are reports that he was able to do impressive—and clearly intelligent—things such as replay any piece of music he'd just heard, recite lengthy passages of Biblical scripture from memory, or speak in rhyming verse.

HUGH MCMANAWAY SCULPTURE

WHAT A golden statue installed in 2000 as a tribute to the man who directed traffic at one of the city's busiest intersections from the 1950s to the 1970s

WHERE The intersection of Queens and Providence Roads

COST Free

PRO TIP Local sculptor Elsie Shaw created the statue. Shaw's other works can be found around the country, as well as just down the street where her Miss Anne & Dan life-size sculpture of a woman with her dog is on the grounds of Queen's University.

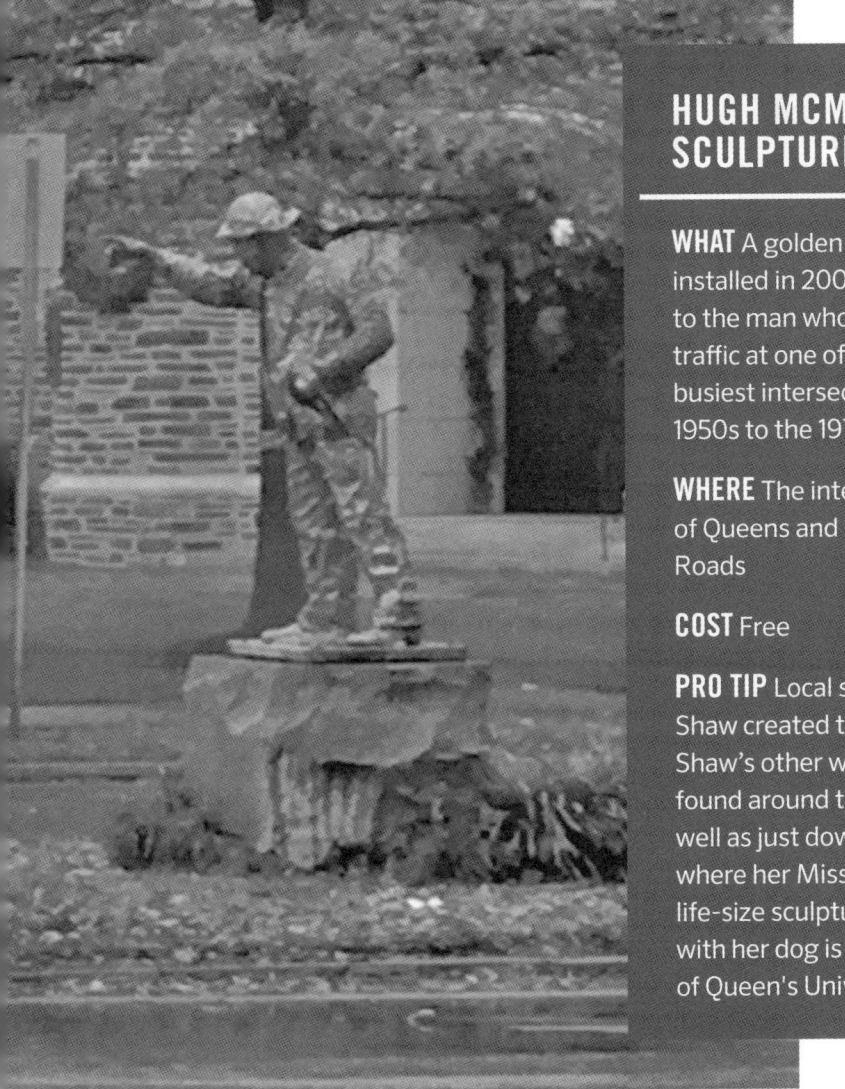

This statue of Hugh McManaway at the corner of Queens and Providence Roads is a tribute to the friendly and beloved local man who stood at the intersection for years, holding his white towel and directing traffic.

known and beloved figure for those passing through the intersection. When McManaway died in 1989, two local sisters wanted to commemorate the friendly man so many recognized. With the help of an Arts and Science Council grant and former Bank of America CEO Hugh McColl, the pair raised funds for a statue honoring the man whose friendly wave many still remember well.

62 THINK PINK

What's with the pink skyscraper in South End?

In a skyline primarily filled with hues of clear and blue, South End's Arlington building stands out. Twenty-two stories of pink glass make up this condominium building that rises above its neighbors.

Completed in 2003, the building has been controversial from the start with its unusual tint garnering it nicknames like "Pepto-Bismol" and "Big Pink." Early renderings show clear and reflective glass, and its developer doesn't speak about the building's design, so it's difficult to say why the ultimate result is a tall and shiny pink building. Many speculate that it was an attempt for the building to blend better with South End's surrounding brick exteriors.

The exact shade of the glass, which does not actually tint the views from the interior, is "Desert Rose." Regardless of what name you deem the shade, the building has faced its fair share of controversy. Not only

---

Jim Gross, who has created developments around Charlotte for decades, was behind The Arlington. Some of his other notable projects include turning the former Ivey's department store building in Uptown into residential housing (before living Uptown was a thing) and, most recently, luxury condo projects in Myers Park and Eastover.

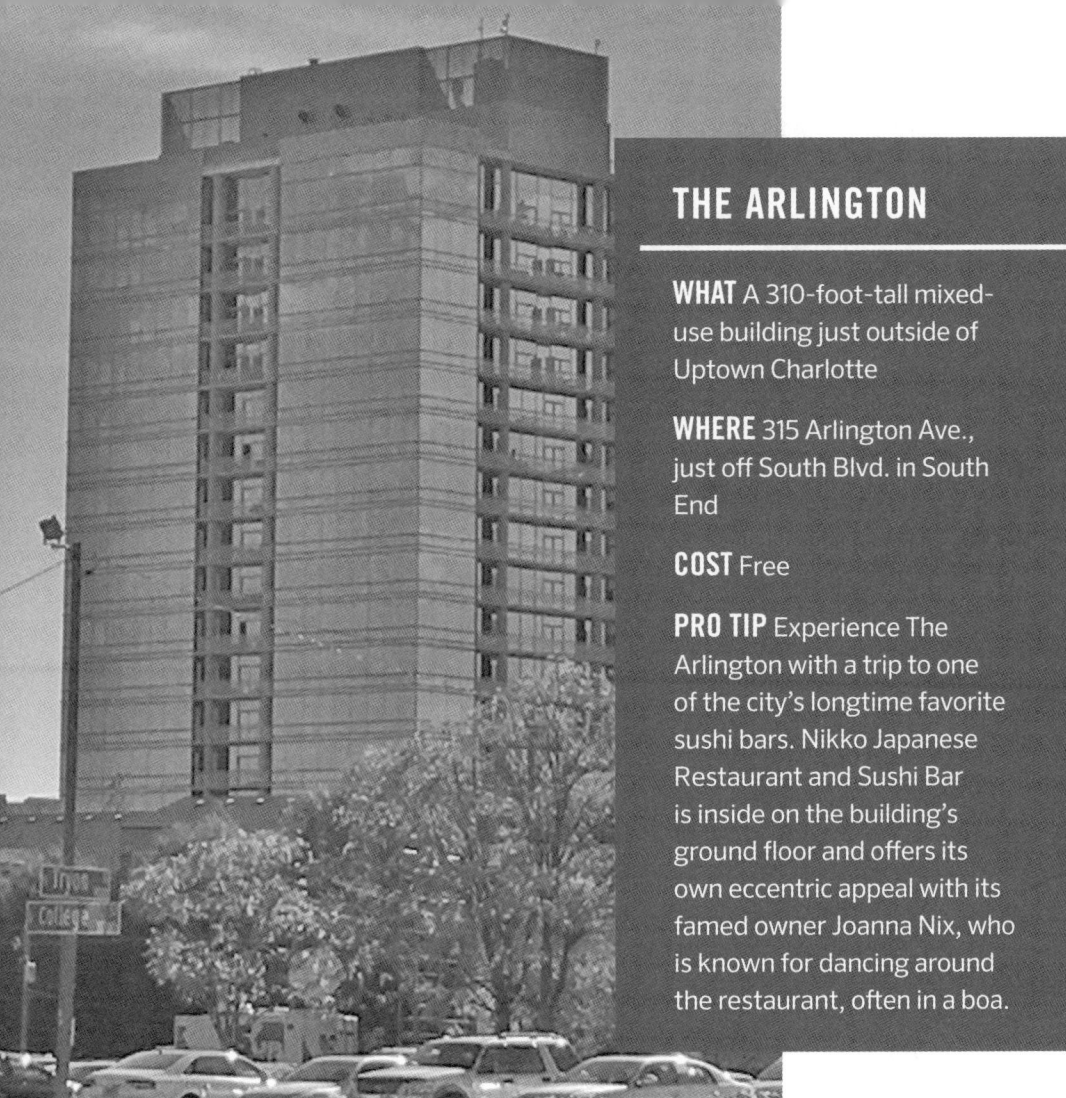

THE ARLINGTON

WHAT A 310-foot-tall mixed-use building just outside of Uptown Charlotte

WHERE 315 Arlington Ave., just off South Blvd. in South End

COST Free

PRO TIP Experience The Arlington with a trip to one of the city's longtime favorite sushi bars. Nikko Japanese Restaurant and Sushi Bar is inside on the building's ground floor and offers its own eccentric appeal with its famed owner Joanna Nix, who is known for dancing around the restaurant, often in a boa.

Some say that the tall pink Arlington Building in South End is an eyesore, while others like its distinctive rose tones.

is its coloring unusual, but it's significantly taller than any other nearby buildings, making it very conspicuous in an otherwise largely residential area.

But the controversy hasn't seemed to stand in the way of the building's popularity with residents, who enjoy some of the city's best skyline views from the north side of the building—and an easily identifiable spot to call home.

63 WORM WORRIES

Why are there bands around tree trunks all over Charlotte?

If you've never lived in a place with cankerworms, then Charlotte's trees must appear to be oddly decorated. Drive through some of the city's most tree-filled neighborhoods like Myers Park or Dilworth during the colder months, and you're likely to see large, thick bands surrounding many of the trunks.

This is actually part of a program the city started in 1990 to protect Charlotte's impressive tree canopy. The city's goal is to increase the current canopy by fifty percent by 2050. But the fall cankerworm, a small caterpillar with a taste for leaves, can weaken and even kill those trees.

The city recommends that trees be banded around November and December. Cankerworms cannot make it

---

Every November the city of Charlotte monitors that year's fall cankerworm population—and then follows up in the spring to monitor any damage done to the city's trees. Despite all efforts to the contrary, Charlotte's cankerworm population continues to grow, but the banding program over the last quarter-century has helped reduce their damage.

QUEENS ROAD WEST

WHAT A stretch of road in Myers Park known for its tall and historic tree canopy, and festooned with adhesive waterproof paper bands from November through February

WHERE Queens Road West between East Blvd. and Queens Road intersections

COST Free

PRO TIP This road is also part of the renowned biking and walking loop, known as the Booty Loop, and a favorite for those on foot.

Myers Park's Queens Road features one of the city's most beautiful tree canaopies, so it's no surprise that its trees are often banded to protect them from infestation by the pesky cankerworms.

across the band and so they're prevented from climbing into the branches to eat leaves or lay eggs.

Many homeowners band their own trees to protect their yard, but the city also has grants that help with the costs for neighborhoods—with everyone banding together to keep Charlotte's trees healthy and beautiful.

64. LIGHT SHOW

What do the different colors of the lights on the Duke Energy Center mean?

The Duke Energy Center is an architectural standout in Charlotte's ever-growing skyline. The forty-eight-floor skyscraper appears to have a bar or handle across its slanted top, and each night the building shines from 507 colorful light fixtures down its side and across the "handle," and often the colors chosen have specific meanings.

The lights were created with the idea of connecting the building to the Charlotte community by showing support for local organizations and people. When it was originally created, there was some mystery behind what the lights might mean, so Wells Fargo Corporate Properties, which manages the lights, created a Twitter account, @flightsclt, for explanations.

> Its lights aren't the only things that make the Duke Energy Center stand out. At forty-eight floors (fifty-four, if you include mechanical floors), it's the second-tallest building in town—and the largest for square footage. It's also LEED-certified, with features such as a system that harvests rainwater for irrigation for the adjoining park.

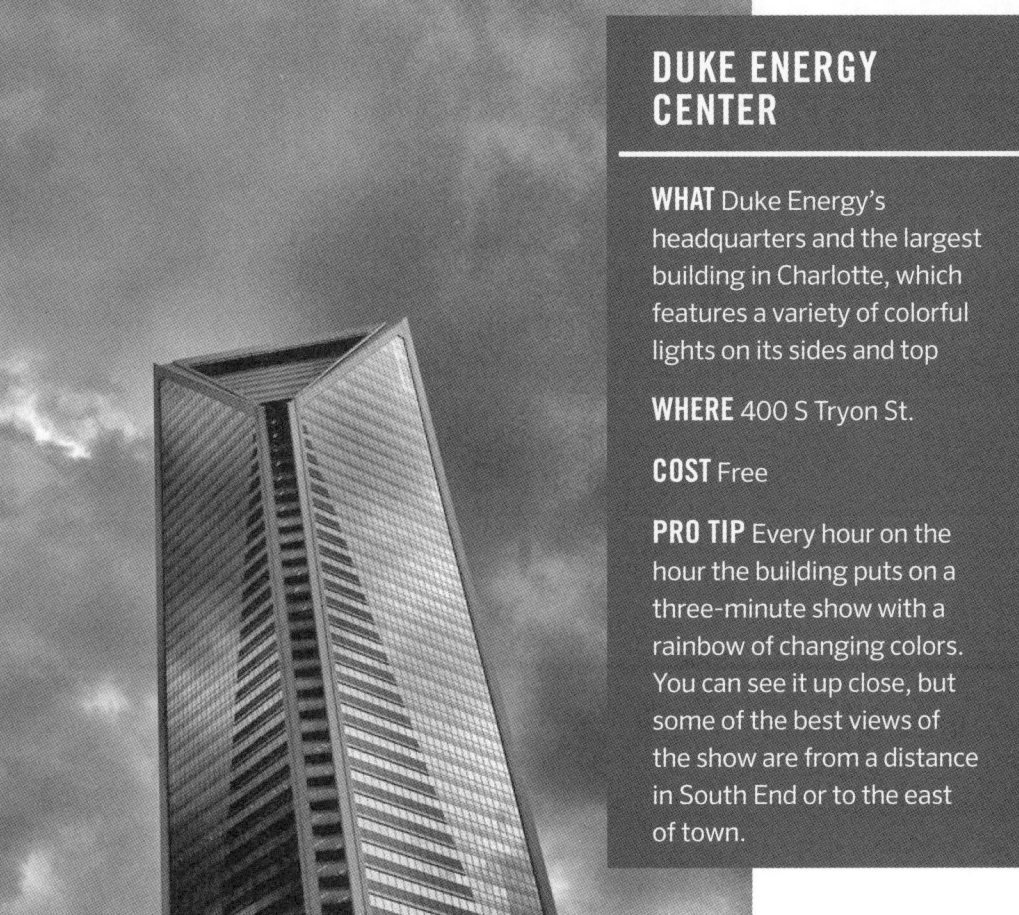

DUKE ENERGY CENTER

WHAT Duke Energy's headquarters and the largest building in Charlotte, which features a variety of colorful lights on its sides and top

WHERE 400 S Tryon St.

COST Free

PRO TIP Every hour on the hour the building puts on a three-minute show with a rainbow of changing colors. You can see it up close, but some of the best views of the show are from a distance in South End or to the east of town.

Uptown's forty-eight-floor Duke Energy building features exterior lights that change colors at night based on events like supporting the Carolina Panthers or local charities.

But there are some color schemes that need no explanation. When the Panthers score a touchdown during a Carolina Panthers game, the bright lights on the side of the building flash blue and white in celebration.

The most impressive part of the light shows however may be the simplicity behind them. The company uses an iPad to program the colors, and it costs less than $5 per night to run the energy-efficient lights.

65 CALIFORNIA DREAMING

Where did UNC Charlotte's 49ers get their name?

There are a variety of stories about why the University of North Carolina at Charlotte decided to take on the 49ers nickname and grizzled "Norm the Niner" gold miner mascot for its athletic teams. Some say that it's because the school's main entrance is located on North Carolina Highway 49. Others say it's related to the school's close proximity to Reed Gold Mine, the country's first major mine. But both of these things seem to be purely coincidental.

Ultimately, the name came from the year 1949, when the recently built campus of UNC Charlotte was saved from being shut down by the state. Bonnie Cone, the university's founder, felt that those students in 1949 had the same resilient and passionate spirit of those who sought fortune in California during its famed gold rush in 1849. So UNC Charlotte became the 49ers in reference to a gold rush that had happened on the other side of the country one hundred years before.

UNC CHARLOTTE

WHAT A public university and the largest institution of higher education in the Charlotte region, with an enrollment just under thirty thousand

WHERE 9201 University City Blvd.

COST Free

PRO TIP The University was originally opened as the Charlotte Center of the University of North Carolina in 1946 and designed to educate returning WWII veterans. It was largely a night school and so, at that time, its athletic teams were known as the Owls.

The University of North Carolina at Charlotte's mascot is Norm the Niner and the team is known as the 49ers—a name that came from the year 1949, when the school was saved from being shut down.

Bonnie Cone is attributed with saving the now-thriving university from being closed in 1949. She began leading the then-dubbed "Charlotte Center of the University of North Carolina" in 1946 and chose the current site for the school. Cone also served as Chancellor of the school until 1966 and after her death in 2003, U.S. Highway 29 near the school was renamed "Dr. Bonnie Cone Memorial Highway."

66 THERE GOES THE NEIGHBORHOOD

How did a popular local music venue replace an X-rated movie theatre?

Before it became the city's artsiest neighborhood, and before craft breweries began popping up along its streets, and long before its craftsman bungalows became popular among the young professional crowd, the NoDa neighborhood had a mixed, and sometimes seedy, past.

Home to numerous textile mills, the mill village thrived during the early part of the twentieth century. The area was three miles from Uptown and developed its own urban center complete with grocery stores, diners, and various other retail establishments, and in 1945 the neighborhood got its first movie theatre, The Astor.

Unfortunately, in the 1960s, the once-flourishing Charlotte textile industry took a dramatic downturn, and by 1975 all of the mills in the area had closed. By then the neighborhood, which had always been lower income,

---

Today, the NoDa neighborhood, which is home to Neighborhood Theatre, is flourishing more than ever. The new light rail line, which will soon run through the neighborhood, has quickly attracted developers, turning former textile mills (the same ones whose shuttering cause the neighborhood downturn in the 1960s) into stylish new shopping and dining venues.

NEIGHBORHOOD THEATRE

WHAT A local performance venue that was once a movie theater

WHERE 511 East 35th St.

COST Varies depending on event

PRO TIP The venue, which holds almost 1,000 people, was recently renovated. Today you'll find a new bar when you enter (filled with craft beers from around the neighborhood) and a modern PA system. But look for remaining touches of the historic space, like its ornate ceiling tiles.

Today, NoDa's Neighborhood Theatre has acted as a music and event space, a farmers market, and even a church. But just a few decades ago the historic theatre was a cinema for X-rated films.

had fallen into disrepair. The Astor had become The Astor Art Cinema and was known as a place to see X-rated films and purchase novelty items.

The cinema eventually closed in the late 1970s as the neighborhood began to go through a transition to a more arts-focused area. Then, in 1997 the theatre was restored, renamed, and converted into a live performance venue—a perfect fit for the growing artsy district.

Since then, Neighborhood theatre has become one of the area's top event and performance venues. From famed musicians to festivals to even Sunday morning church services, the historic theatre still draws crowds more than a half a century later.

67 PEEK AT THE PAST

Why was a child's coffin once uncovered at what is now Midtown's Metropolitan shopping center?

If you've ever picked up groceries in the Midtown Trader Joe's, grabbed a bite at one of Metropolitan's numerous restaurants, or strolled along Little Sugar Creek Greenway near Charlottetown Avenue, then you've walked on hallowed ground from Charlotte's ever-evolving history. In 1959, the Charlottetown Mall opened on that spot as the first enclosed and air-conditioned shopping center in the Southeast.

At its October opening, which included a band and speeches for an estimated crowd of fifty thousand people, a time capsule was buried that included editions of *The Charlotte Observer*, predictions for the future, and radio recordings. When the capsule was dug up in 1984, much had changed, including the addition of other larger enclosed malls like SouthPark and Eastland.

Charlotte, as it turns out, loves its time capsules. The ones from Midtown's mall weren't the only ones around town. In 2014, for example, Charlotte officials opened a fifty-year-old capsule that had been buried at the Regal Park Terrace theater. Unfortunately, it had met the same fate as the original Charlottetown version—moisture had made a mess of its historical offerings.

A stroll down Little Sugar Creek Greenway today takes you past the Metropolitan complex filled with shops and restaurants. But in the past, this lush area and its creek were covered by a historic shopping mall.

LITTLE SUGAR CREEK GREENWAY

WHAT The greenway that runs adjacent to the Metropolitan development along Little Sugar Creek

WHERE The greenway will ultimately be part of a 19-mile project, but to experience the area that was formerly Charlottetown Mall, walk on its path between 7th St. and Morehead St.

COST Free

PRO TIP When Charlottetown Mall existed, its parking lot covered up what is now the greenway, stretching over Little Sugar Creek, which ran in a tunnel beneath it. The mall's cinema, which was across Charlottetown Ave., had a parking lot that closely bordered the creek.

The capsule, which was actually a small child's coffin, had unfortunately become moist inside and most of its contents were damaged, so the owners tried again—this time burying a capsule to be opened in 2009. That capsule, according to the now defunct *Charlotte News*, included items from the period, such as bobby socks and sunglasses, as well as future predictions from local students.

Of course by 2009 even more had changed. The mall had become Outlet Square and then Midtown Square before being demolished and rebuilt as the now modern Metropolitan. The capsule is said to have been uncovered by the center's developer Pappas Properties, but has never officially been opened for the public.

68 FIND THE SHINE

Why does one of Uptown's most modern buildings have an authentic moonshine still inside?

Uptown's NASCAR Hall of Fame may be housed in one of the city's newest and most modern skyscrapers, but many of its souvenir items offer a colorful look at the region's history. And while you'd expect to find plenty of famed cars and automobile paraphernalia, what you might not anticipate seeing is an authentic moonshine still.

However, famed driver Junior Johnson, who is well known for his years running moonshine, contributed the large still for the exhibit. Made of wood, metal, and copper, the still includes two boilers and a cooker among other parts. It's only fitting that Johnson himself constructed the still as moonshine was, after all, his family business.

Johnson first ran moonshine as a fourteen-year-old. He later served time in federal prison for producing the liquor, and like many of the original drivers, it was his years of outrunning the police that led to his career in the

---

Moonshine has become a popular addition to many local cocktails in recent years, offering a historical—and potent—taste of the region. Possibly most notable is TEN Park Lanes, a retro bowling alley-meets-restaurant that serves a variety of moonshine flavors on tap.

At the NASCAR Hall of Fame in Uptown Charlotte guests can peruse historic cars and memorabilia, and learn about the sport of NASCAR's past and present.

sport of automobile racing. From winning numerous races to helping to push the sport in front of the public eye, Johnson's illustrious and influential career ultimately earned him a place as one of the first five Hall of Fame inductees. You can learn more about him in the museum's Hall of Honor.

NASCAR HALL OF FAME

WHAT An interactive museum dedicated to the sport of NASCAR

WHERE 400 E Martin Luther King Blvd.

COST Tickets are $19.95 for adults

PRO TIP You can enjoy exhibits like Glory Road, a banked ramp featuring 18 historic cars, or the high-octane theater offering interesting NASCAR stories. But if you want a true taste of Junior Johnson's flavor, head to a local ABC store to purchase Midnight Moon produced (legally) by Piedmont Distillers where Junior Johnson is a part owner.

69 'TIS THE SEASON

Why does Charlotte have a giant singing Christmas tree?

The first recorded appearance of a singing Christmas tree was in 1933 at Belhaven University. The "trees," which are generally made of steel and built so that anywhere from thirty to four hundred and fifty singers can stand on them, have since been constructed at churches and in communities around the world.

Charlotte's first singing Christmas tree performance was in 1954. One of the performers had seen the Belhaven tree and liked the idea, so when the Charlotte Choral Society formed that year, they held the first tree program on Providence Road. The next year, a larger tree was constructed, and in 1955 the full production was showcased in the newly built Ovens Auditorium.

Today, after more than sixty years of annual caroling performances, it's still a breathtaking experience when the curtain opens to reveal a thirty-two-foot-tall

---

ANNUAL SINGING CHRISTMAS TREE

WHAT A family-friendly program featuring the singing tree as well as puppets, dancers, and, of course, Santa

WHERE The Knight Theater, 430 S Tryon St.

COST Ticket prices start at $13

PRO TIP If you're taking younger children, opt for the Singing Christmas Tree for Kids, which features a shorter version of the performance and is focused on its more playful holiday aspects.

For more than six decades Carolina Voices has presented its singing Christmas tree each year to celebrate the holiday season. Guests can purchase tickets to the performances, which are now held in Uptown's Knight Theater.

tree holding one hundred singers amidst sparkling lights and decorations. The height and the heat from the stage lights can make this difficult for some singers, who often even wear shorts behind the green faux branches. But this doesn't stop them from performing all of your favorite Christmas tunes, from classics to pop.

The kid-friendly version of Charlotte's singing Christmas tree only lasts one hour, and the performance includes extra playful touches like puppets, a children's choir, a purple hippo, and, of course, an appearance by Santa Claus.

70 MYSTERY BUILDING ON BREVARD

Why has a row house built in 1887 sat vacant for decades among Uptown's skyscrapers?

William Treloar was a British gold miner who moved to Charlotte and owned a hotel here in the 1840s. But when the Civil War began, Treloar moved his family to Philadelphia and didn't return until 1886. At the time, Uptown's Brevard Street was filled with row houses as part of its First Ward neighborhood. Treloar and his wife, Julie, built their own Victorian home on the street in 1887 for the price of $2,500.

Unfortunately, Treloar died just a few years later, in 1894. The house remained in the family for several years before starting to go through various owners. It has been a rental property, an auto parts company, and even a bail bond company. Then, in the late 1990s, Levine Properties purchased the home.

The Wall Poems Project isn't the first time the William Treloar House has been used for public art. In 2013, a project called Inside Out 11M, which was designed to promote immigration reform, took the photos of individual Charlotteans smiling and waving. They then printed the photos and pasted them in the windows of the home.

THE WILLIAM TRELOAR HOUSE

WHAT A historic home in Uptown Charlotte

WHERE 328 N Brevard St.

COST Free (not open to the public)

PRO TIP If you enjoy the poetry mural, there are many more in the neighborhood. The Wall Poems project features snippets of poetry painted onto Uptown landmarks (www.wallpoems.com).

The William Treloar House, which is located on North Brevard Street in Uptown Charlotte, has been vacant for many years. But you'll see signs of life on its façade, which features a poem from the local Wall Poems project.

Since then, the home has sat vacant. A local arts group wrote poetry and drew on its brick walls, and one of its windows held a camera that filmed a time lapse of the new Google Fiber building being developed across the street. These days, as the area around it develops with First Ward Park and UNC Charlotte's Uptown campus, there's talk of it becoming a restaurant, which seems fitting. Treloar and his wife built it as a home for their thirteen children, which means this wouldn't be the first time this was a gathering place for groups around a table.

71. HOLY GROUNDS

How did an official Catholic pilgrimage shrine come to be built just outside of Charlotte?

In 1876, Benedictine monks from Saint Vincent Abbey opened Saint Mary's College on a former farm in what is now Belmont, just to the west of Charlotte. Today, the college is known as Belmont Abbey and, while driving on I-85, you've likely noticed its distinct gothic revival architecture in what is otherwise a typical Southern suburban area.

The college stands out simply for being a Catholic school in a heavily Protestant region. It has Benedictine monks who don't take a vow of silence, but do follow the teachings of the sixth-century St. Benedict. One of its most unusual aspects in this fairly rural area of North Carolina is the Grotto of Our Lady of Lourdes, a shrine that was built in 1891.

The story of its construction begins in 1890, when it's said that one of the monks at the school was stricken with typhoid fever. The other monks were praying daily and decided that intercession of the Blessed Virgin Mary was needed. It was resolved that if the monk's health

---

The library at Belmont Abbey also offers insight into both the school and religion's history. It includes monastic and Benedictine books, books on the region, and a large selection of rare volumes.

GROTTO OF OUR LADY OF LOURDES

WHAT A grotto modeled after the cave at Lourdes featuring a terra-cotta statue of the Virgin Mary

WHERE Belmont Abbey College, 100 Belmont Mount Holly Rd., Belmont, NC

COST Free

PRO TIP The grotto is outside and includes benches and kneelers in front of it. While you're there, you can experience the surrounding gardens that are maintained by the monks as well as the Basilica of Mary Help of Christians, which has stained glass windows that were exhibited at the World's Fair in 1892.

Tucked on the grounds of Belmont Abbey College is a grotto that honors Our Lady of Lourdes. The shrine was built as a way of thanksgiving in 1891.

returned, they would build a grotto in honor of Our Lady in thanksgiving. According to the story, the sick monk was quickly healed and construction began.

The Grotto was placed on the National Register of Historic Places in 1953, and today it's one of many Grottos of Our Lady of Lourdes around the world.

72 TAKE IT TO THE BANK

Why is there a stagecoach from 1855 in Uptown Charlotte?

In a city known for its banking industry, it's not surprising to see a museum dedicated to one of its largest financial institutions, Wells Fargo Bank. But the original Wells Fargo stagecoach, built by Lewis Downing Co. in 1855 and sitting in the front window of an Uptown building, will definitely catch your eye.

The six-thousand-square-foot museum, which is dedicated to the history of Wells Fargo, has a heavy emphasis on memorabilia from Wachovia, the North Carolina bank it purchased in 2008. There's a desk that was used by former Wachovia CEOs and a model of an 1889 Wachovia Bank branch.

The museum offers a variety of interactive exhibits including having your photo printed on fake money or going through a drive-through bank with working tubes. But one of its most fun options is climbing inside a replica of a stagecoach, which rocks back and forth and features movie scenes of passing landscapes.

Charlotte isn't the only spot where Wells Fargo operates a museum. If you're up for traveling, you can learn more about the company's history at the Pony Express Terminal in Sacramento, at the Alaska Heritage Museum in Anchorage, and at its museum in Old Town San Diego State Historic Park.

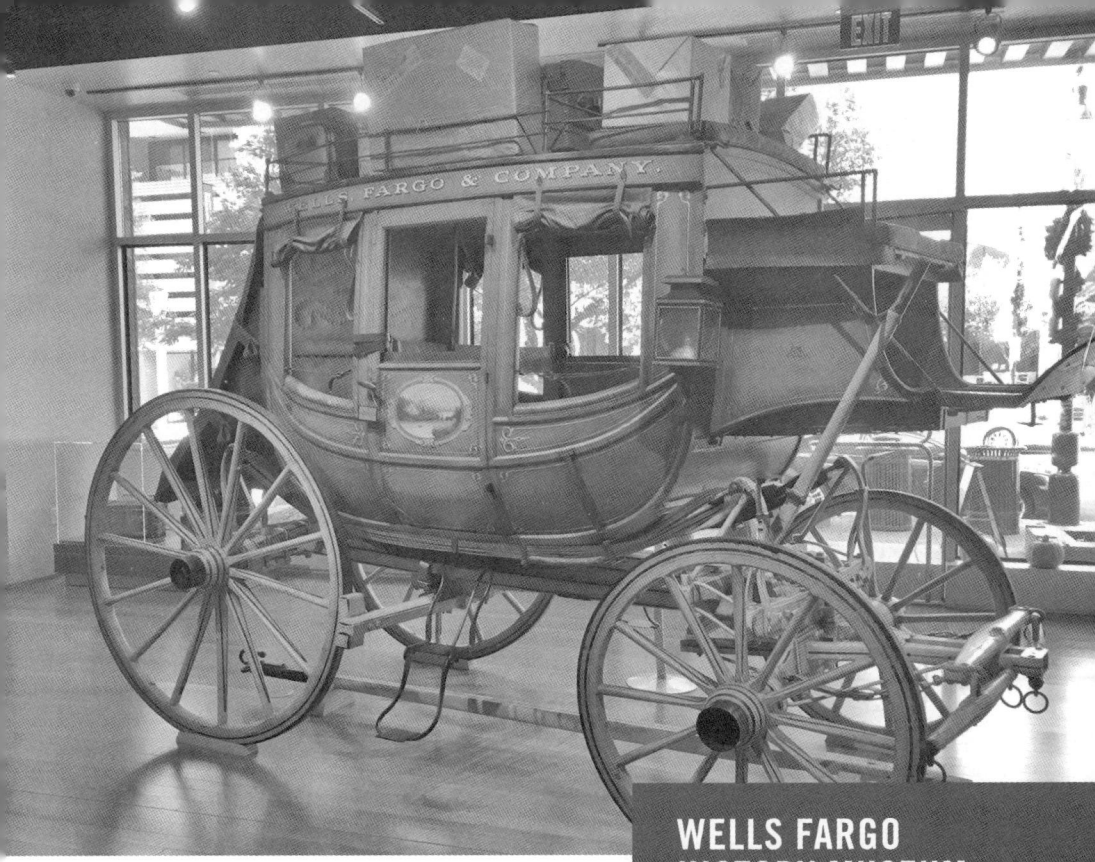

Inside the Wells Fargo History Museum on South Tryon Street are various pieces of memorabilia sharing the story of the bank's past, most notably this 1855 stagecoach.

WELLS FARGO HISTORY MUSEUM

WHAT A small museum dedicated to the history of Wells Fargo Bank, especially as it has affected North Carolina

WHERE 401 S Tryon St.

COST Free

PRO TIP This free museum is small, but it's a great stop for kids. From playing with interactive displays to sitting in the stagecoach, all of the exhibits are family-friendly.

73 PRESIDENTIAL SEAL OF DISAPPROVAL

Why was President George Washington dismissive of Charlotte?

In 1791, President George Washington was taking a tour of the South and stopped for a night in Charlotte. More than five hundred people lined the streets to greet the President as he arrived for dinner at Colonel Thomas Polk's home, which was on the northeast corner of Trade and Tryon Streets in the center of Uptown.

That night, he stayed at Cook's Inn across the street. When he departed the following day, he left behind a box of white wig powder, which it's said that Mrs. Cook would occasionally put on children's hair and say to them that they had the President's powder in their hair.

If, as a Charlottean, you're feeling insulted by Washington's description of the city circa 1791 as "a very trifling place," don't despair. Charlotte wasn't the only spot the first President deemed trifling. One month earlier, on his travels through Greenville, NC, he'd described it in the exact same manner.

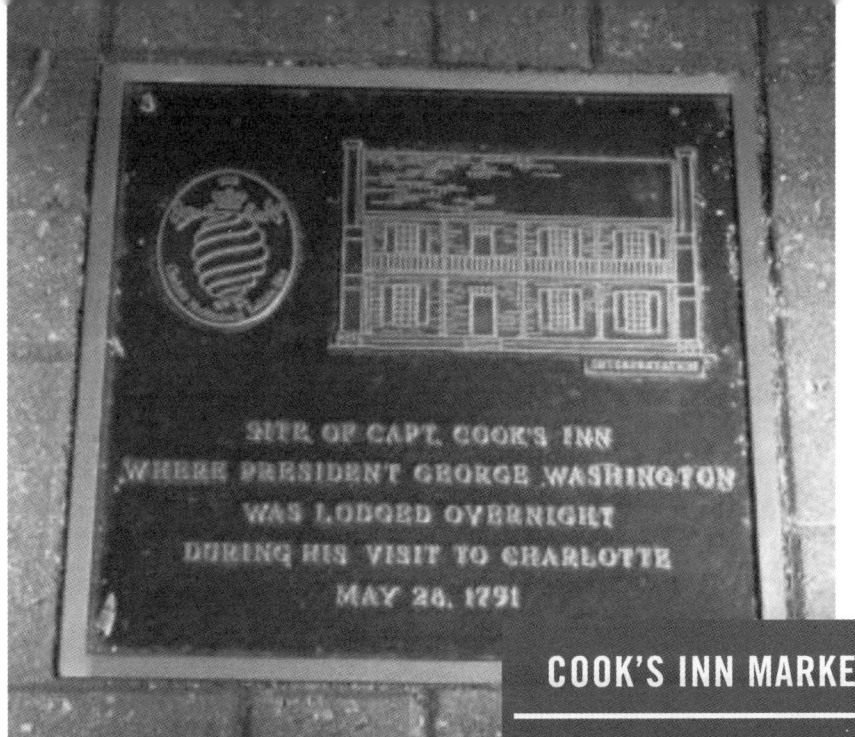

This plaque in Uptown marks the spot where President George Washington stayed overnight on his travels through Charlotte in 1791, when he famously called the city a "trifling place."

Unfortunately, President Washington wasn't as enamored with Charlotte as the city seemed to be with him. In his journal, he wrote, "Charlotte is a very trifling place, though the Court of Mecklenburg is held in it."

COOK'S INN MARKER

WHAT A historic marker commemorating the site of Cook's Inn, where President Washington stayed on the night of May 28, 1791

WHERE On the south side of Trade Street, just to the west of the intersection with Tryon

COST Free

PRO TIP Diagonally across the street you'll find the site of Colonel Thomas Polk's home, where President Washington dined during his trip. Or, to learn more about Polk, visit the adjacent Thomas Polk Park, which features stones offering details about his many accomplishments.

74 EXOTIC EXPERIENCE

Why do giraffes, deer, and ostrich all live together on a farm just north of Charlotte?

About half an hour north of Charlotte is Lazy 5 Ranch, an attraction that kids love—and even parents secretly enjoy. The 185-acre ranch is almost entirely drive-through. Visitors buy buckets of animal feed on their way in and then reach out their windows during the 3.5-mile drive, offering the feed to the farm's many animals.

Perhaps the most incredible thing about Lazy 5 Ranch, though, is the story behind it. Henry Hampton, who had been raising exotic animals for decades, noticed that often passersby paused in his driveway hoping to get a glimpse of the animals. He began hosting school groups, who would gaze at the creatures through the fence.

He decided that he wanted people to have a closer experience. And so, in 1993, he opened the Lazy 5 Ranch, playfully named for the five people in his family at that time. It's a completely private zoo with no federal or state

---

It may be tempting to stay in your own car for the ride through the ranch, but be forewarned: Things get a little messy. When you're feeding large animals through the window of your car, it's very likely that you're going to end up with (many) pieces of the food falling inside your vehicle.

LAZY 5 RANCH

WHAT A drive-through petting zoo experience featuring a mix of exotic animals

WHERE 15100 Highway 150 East

COST Admission is $11 for adults, $8 for children. Animal feed is $3 per bucket. The ranch does not accept credit cards.

PRO TIP While all of the other animals on the ranch can be fed by hand, guests are asked not to feed the zebras. This is because zebras have teeth on both the bottom and top of their mouths, while the other animals on the ranch do not have potentially dangerous teeth. In other words, zebras can bite.

At the Lazy 5 Ranch in Mooresville, guests can feed and pet animals like ostrich, deer, and even giraffes like this one.

funding. In addition to allowing people to drive through, guests can opt for a horse-drawn wagon ride, which allows for an even closer-up experience of the more than 750 animals that call the farm home.

75 THE SCOOP ON THE COOP

Why does one Charlotte restaurant serve its chicken sandwiches with the bone in?

When Price's Chicken Coop opened in South End Charlotte, it was a different city. In 1962, the neighborhood was full of factories, and this small take-out spot opened as a place for industrial workers to grab a bite at lunch. Things have changed a lot on the street since then.

Now, the small restaurant is surrounded by upscale boutiques and dining. It faces the tracks for the LYNX light rail. Smaller buildings on its street have been replaced with tall, new apartments. But Price's hasn't changed.

Inside the restaurant you'll find white cinder block walls, a row of fryers, and a sign that reads "cash only." It's still takeout, which now means that people hurry back to their cars with the cardboard boxes of food. And, of course, it's the food—specifically, the tender fried chicken—that's caused this place to have daily long lines down the sidewalk for more than half a century.

Despite its blue collar roots and casual vibe, Price's has become a favorite for visiting celebrities. Comedian Jay Leno has chowed down on a wing dinner in the grass across the street from the restaurant, and visiting NFL and NBA players often stop in for the boxed meals.

Known as a favorite spot for visiting celebrities (Jay Leno loves the fried chicken), Price's Chicken Coop in South End has been serving up its casual take-out boxed meals since 1962.

PRICE'S CHICKEN COOP

WHAT A take-out restaurant in South End known for its fresh fried chicken

WHERE 11614 Camden Rd.

COST The prices here are inexpensive, with a ¼ chicken dinner including cole slaw, French fries, hushpuppies, and a roll going for $7.50.

PRO TIP Don't wait until you drive all the way home or back to the office for this. There's a good reason you'll see people sitting on the curb or in their cars digging in to this warm, fried chicken. It's best fresh out of the fryer.

The chicken is cut in-house, leaving a breast bone in so that the meat stays moist. It's coated in seasoned flour and then fried in peanut oil. And whether you order it in pieces or on a sandwich, the bone stays in.

76 LOOKING UP

Why is the entire text of *The Art of War* painted on the ceiling of an Uptown restaurant?

One of Charlotte's most popular restaurants sits on the corner of 5th and Church Streets. 5Church, whose chef has been a contestant on Top Chef, was such a success in the Queen City that its owners have opened the concept in both Atlanta and Charleston—with plans for more on the way.

And while the food is impressive and the bar's nightlife scene is one of the best in town, it may be the décor that makes this restaurant exceptional. On the ceiling of 5Church you'll find the entire (yes, all forty thousand words) text of Sun Tzu's two-thousand-year-old military treatise *The Art of War*, hand-painted in white lettering on a black ceiling.

It took local artist Jon Norris more than three months on ladders to complete the exposed ceiling. He held a brush in one hand, the book in the other, and the paint in a container he'd tied to his finger. The idea came from Mills Howell, one of the owners, who is also part owner of an interior design

---

The ceiling isn't the only creative aspect of 5Church's design. The rustic-meets-modern tables in the bar area are made of Himalayan oak and lined with Lucite chairs. White and feathery chandeliers hang over the bar. Black leather tufted couches create a living room vibe near the windows. And a giant five dollar bill image lines one wall.

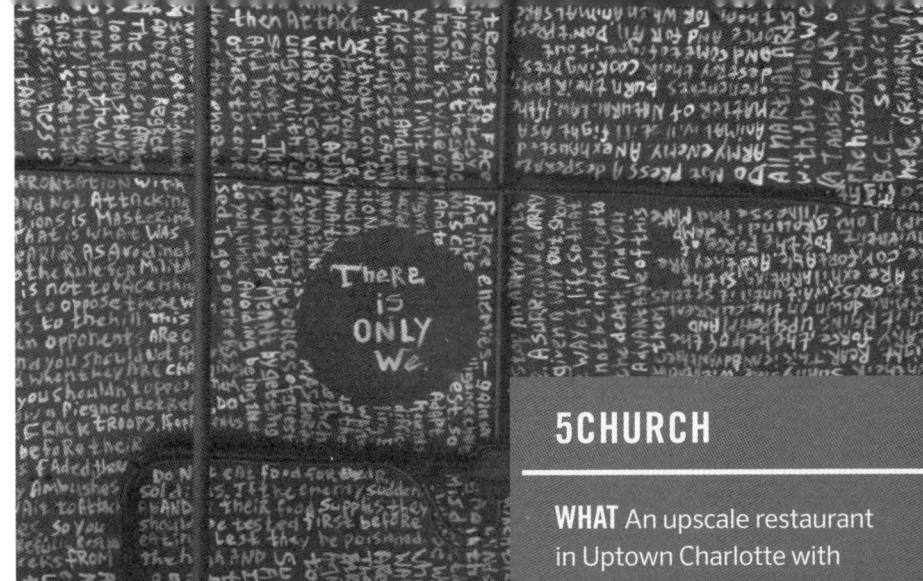

Uptown's sleek 5Church restaurant features a celebrity chef, award-winning fare, and one of the city's chicest interiors—complete with the entire text of The Art of War *on its ceiling.*

5CHURCH

WHAT An upscale restaurant in Uptown Charlotte with *The Art of War* painted on its ceiling

WHERE Corner of 5th and Church Streets in Uptown

COST Prices vary, with dinner entrees starting around $20

PRO TIP If you're not in the mood for a full meal but want to check out the ceiling, snag a stool at the bar. The restaurant has an impressive wine list as well as tasty cocktails like the spicy Viper, made with tequila, orange liqueur, lime juice, cucumber water, and cayenne pepper.

firm. The group had been quoting the ancient classic so much as they went through the strenuous process of opening the first restaurant in 2012, they thought its words should be over their heads as they worked.

Now, the eye-catching design is the restaurant's signature ceiling. Guests at 5Church's restaurants in Charleston and Atlanta can also look up and read the hand-painted text.

77 THE BIG HEAD

Why is there a giant head sculpture in the front yard of a home on The Plaza?

Today, Plaza Midwood is full of trendy shops, stylish restaurants, and hip nightlife. Its bungalows and historic homes are owned by young professionals and families. But twenty years ago, the neighborhood just to the east of Charlotte was an urban and eclectic mix of artists and workers who really created its popular vibe.

In 1986, photographer Jim McGuire was one of those artists. He purchased a home on the neighborhood's main road, The Plaza. The home is charming with plenty of curbside appeal, and McGuire decided it needed something a little more distinctive.

In 2005, he got "The Head," a six-foot tall sculpture of a face that had been used by a theater group called the Moving Poets. With its raised eyebrows and open mouth, the face appears to be either scared or shocked. Whatever its emotion, it's a startling sight to the viewer who stumbles upon it for the first time.

For another look at local artistic expression in Plaza Midwood, stop by Twenty-Two. The bar and gallery, just a few blocks from "The Head," brings new art exhibits from local and national artists each month—and offers wine, craft beer, and sake in its sleek and modern space.

Plaza Midwood has plenty of artistic roots in its past, so it should come as no surprise that a home on its main residential street, The Plaza, would have something as unusual as a giant face sculpture in its front yard.

THE HEAD SCULPTURE

WHAT A large statue of a head in a Plaza Midwood front yard

WHERE 1415 The Plaza

COST Free

PRO TIP Continue your walk up The Plaza to check out other interesting neighborhood destinations, including the yellow two-story Queen Anne Victorian home across the street that was built in 1889 in Uptown Charlotte. It was moved between 1910 and 1920 to its current location and is now a designated historic landmark.

78. CLAIM TO FAME

Why did actors Claire Danes and Damian Lewis play pool in a pub called the Fat Parrot?

Charlotte has plenty of places that have been chosen as the sets for internationally renowned films and television shows. After all, much of *The Hunger Games* was filmed here, as well as hit shows like Fox's *Sleepy Hollow* and Showtime's *Homeland*. But most of the sites for filming were well known spots like Uptown's Marshall Park or Knight Theater, or Myers Park's Duke Mansion.

There were, however, a few more out-of-the-way places that got their fifteen minutes of fame when the location scouts discovered them. One of those places is a local pub called the Fat Parrot. It's in the Mountain Island area on Mount Holly-Huntersville Road (not exactly where you'd expect to find Hollywood stars).

In Season One of the award-winning *Homeland* series, the show's two main characters, Brody (played by Damian Lewis) and Carrie (played by Claire Danes), play a game of pool that ultimately turns into a bar fight. Apparently, the Fat Parrot with its laid-back vibe, gravel parking lot, and cold beer was the perfect place for this scene, which you'll find in Episode Seven.

T'S FAT PARROT

WHAT An unassuming bar offering drinks and games like cornhole, pool, and darts

WHERE 5416 Mount Holly-Huntersville Rd.

COST Food and drinks are inexpensive

PRO TIP There's live music on Saturday nights.

When Emmy-award winning Showtime series Homeland *launched, it was filming in Charlotte. In one scene its two main characters played a game of pool in this off-the-beaten-path bar.*

Fan of Homeland? There are plenty of other Charlotte spots to explore where the popular show was filmed. Ed's Tavern in Dilworth repeatedly shows up as Brody's favorite watering hole, while Carrie spends an evening in the Ritz-Carlton's lobby lounge. In fact, the Ritz' rooms, bathrooms, spa, pool, and ballroom all make an appearance on the show.

79 HEADS UP

Why do hundreds of small heads hang in the center of the county courthouse?

If you're in the courthouse, chances are you aren't pausing to soak in the artwork—but you should. Hanging in the main atrium of Uptown's Charlotte-Mecklenburg County Courthouse is one of the area's most impressive pieces of art.

Installed in 2007, *Persistence of Vision* changes each week. On Monday, it's a cloud of small and shiny pewter heads that are actually portraits of Charlotte citizens. It hangs from the ceiling on thin cables far above the atrium. Then, as the week goes on, sixteen hundred motors slowly move and shift the heads so that they form a three-dimensional human face hanging over the space. Then the face dissolves and the work begins again the following week.

Each time, the face is different—from a young African American man to an elderly Latina woman. The concept, which was created by Ralph Helmick and Stuart Schechter, is designed to show Charlotte's diversity, both through the small, pewter heads and through the final product—an allegory that's especially fitting in the center for the city's justice.

MECKLENBURG COUNTY COURTHOUSE

WHAT The county courthouse

WHERE 832 E Fourth St.

COST It's free to get in, but you must go through a metal detector

PRO TIP If you're only visiting once, go toward the end of the week, when the face is closer to completely forming.

Each day this sculpture hanging from the ceiling inside Uptown's courthouse changes slightly such that it starts as a cloud of small heads on Monday and ends the week as a 3-D human face.

Ralph Helmick, the artist behind *Persistence of Vision,* has his work featured in public spaces around the country. Helmick created another one of his pieces here in Charlotte at Uptown's McColl Center for Art + Innovation. During a three-month residency there, Helmick designed a sculpture using instruments that measure time to form a portrait of physicist Werner Heisenberg.

80 SIT. STAY. DRINK.

Why does Charlotte have a bar designed specifically for dogs?

If man's best friend is also your best friend, you're in luck. On North Davidson Street in the NoDa neighborhood there is a place called The Dog Bar. The bar is dedicated to social time for and with dogs. For the human guests, there's beer, spirits, and wine (sorry, no food) as well as flat screen televisions and games like cornhole.

But here, the four-legged guests are the stars of the show. The entire bar is fenced in so that dogs can run and play off-leash both inside and outdoors. Inside is climate-controlled for those especially hot or cold days, while outdoors has Astroturf flooring under a shaded patio that features a misting system in the summer and heat in the winter.

The concept was created by J.P. Brewer, who owns two dog daycare and boarding facilities. Brewer, who works with dog rescue and fundraising, thought that dog owners would enjoy a place where both they and their pets could hang out together. Of course, having a dog isn't required in order to visit, but you'll definitely need to like dogs if you're going to be grabbing a drink at this particular watering hole.

THE DOG BAR

WHAT A bar dedicated to being dog-friendly

WHERE 3307 N Davidson St.

COST It's free for people to get in, but there's a $10 annual membership fee for each dog

PRO TIP Keep an eye on the bar's Facebook page for amusing events like a Howl O Ween party with dressed up pups or an ugly sweater Christmas party where everyone participates.

Canines aren't just welcome, they're the star of the show at this NoDa bar featuring dog treats, water bowls, and props for your furry friends.

Dog Bar isn't the only NoDa spot that's canine friendly. The eclectic neighborhood is known for having some of the best breweries in town, and many of them welcome furry friends. Bring Fido along for craft brew spots like Free Range or NoDa Brewing Company.

81 MAKING WAVES

What historic Native American trail lies beneath the U.S. National Whitewater Center?

Anyone who has spent a sunny afternoon at the U.S. National Whitewater Center can appreciate its appeal. Just outside of town and along the Catawba River, the center features eleven hundred acres designed for playing and relaxing. From rafting on the world's largest man-made whitewater river to zip-lining over said river, there's plenty to keep guests entertained.

But hiking and crossing the river in this area weren't always for recreational purposes. The Tuckaseegee Trail, which was one of the Carolina's most traveled Native American paths, once ran through the property. The trail, which also brought European settlers and travelers into Charlotte, is likely one of the major reasons the city initially developed at all.

The trail led to the Tuckaseegee Ford, which is known as the oldest crossing point along the Catawba, and had several historic crossings, including General Rutherford and his troops during the Revolutionary War. And while other routes

---

The U.S. National Whitewater Center's Canopy Tours offer the chance to explore portions of the historic trail and ford in the woods along the Catawba River. The tours, which can be as high as 60 feet in the air, include moving from platform to platform between the trees using zips, nets, and rappels.

The U.S. National Whitewater Center, which was built on the site of a Native American path called the Tuckaseegee Trail, features a variety of recreational activities from whitewater rafting and kayaking to ziplining and ropes courses.

U.S. NATIONAL WHITEWATER CENTER

WHAT A recreational and athletic training facility featuring whitewater, rock climbing, zip-lining, mountain biking, canoeing, and more

WHERE 5000 Whitewater Center Pkwy.

COST It's $5 per car to park, but admission to the center is free. Activity prices vary.

PRO TIP The center pays homage to its past with one of its most popular festivals, the annual Tuck Fest. Named for the Tuckaseegee Ford and Trail, the weekend outdoor festival kicks of the summer season at the center each year.

sprang up along the Catawba, the ford actually remained in use until 1914, when the river was damned to create Lake Wylie, raising the water by twenty feet.

Today, on one of the center's canopy tours, you can explore the area that was once the trail leading to the Ford. And if you paddle around the island in the Catawba on one of the center's kayaks, then you've crossed what was once the Ford.

82 HIDDEN PATH

Why does a wide sidewalk run through the Elizabeth neighborhood with no streets around it?

In the early part of the twentieth century, residents in Charlotte's neighborhoods relied on the streetcar lines in order to commute into Uptown. The system of streetcars around town spurred development and made the homes along the streets where the trolleys ran the most desirable for their convenience.

One of those streets was 7th, where a streetcar line ran out of Uptown, up Elizabeth Avenue, down Hawthorne Lane, and up 7th Street, ending at Clarice Avenue. As developers worked on the Rosemont subdivision of Elizabeth, they had the idea to create the Trolley Walk. This public stretch of sidewalk would make it more convenient for those who lived on the side streets to access the trolley at its terminus—something that would make the homes on those streets more valuable.

The trolley line that the Trolley Walk once connected to is being revived today as the Gold Line streetcar. However, its route is being changed. Now, instead of turning up 7th Street on its way out of town, it will cross 7th on Hawthorne and continue across the Independence Boulevard bridge to Central Avenue.

This path in the Elizabeth neighborhood is so small you might miss it. The walkway, called the Trolley Walk, was originally built to give those in the neighborhood easier access to the then nearby trolley line.

THE TROLLEY WALK

WHAT A walkway that connects East Fifth St. and East Seventh St. in the Elizabeth neighborhood

WHERE It can be entered from 7th St. across the street from Clarice Ave

COST Free

PRO TIP While there are some lights along the path, it's best to check this out during the day.

By the 1930s, streetcars were no longer in fashion and the system closed. And by the 1950s the main streets had become congested and noisy, actually making their homes less valuable. Today, the Trolley Walk is one of the few remnants of the time when streetcars were changing the way the city worked and lived. And while local residents may not use it to walk to the streetcar, its attractive hedges and well-kept path still make it a popular spot for a stroll.

83 ON TRACK

How did Charlotte's race car drivers like its first wooden speedway?

These days when racing fans go to watch the cars sprint around the track at Charlotte Motor Speedway, they're sitting in a venue that holds 94,000 people and includes a 1.5 mile paved asphalt track that's considered the home track for NASCAR.

But Charlotte—and the sport of racing—have come a long way. The first Charlotte Speedway was actually on the town's south side in what's now Pineville. It opened in 1924 and featured a track made of 2 x 4 wooden boards, which were actually considered an improvement over the dirt tracks of the past.

Initially, the track was a huge success. Its first event drew more than fifty thousand people to watch a 250-mile race around the banked mile-long oval with cars hitting speeds

---

Wooden track racing wasn't just popular in Charlotte. There were similar tracks around the country, from Los Angeles to Pennsylvania in the 1910s and 1920s. However, most of the tracks required too much maintenance and only lasted a few years before being abandoned. And by 1932 there were no more championship level races on United States board tracks.

Charlotte's first track, which was made of wooden boards, was located at South Boulevard and I-485—and is long gone. But you can get a taste of the city's racing history like this notorious car at Uptown's NASCAR Hall of Fame.

SOUTH BOULEVARD AND I-485

WHAT The area that was once home to Charlotte's original speedway

WHERE The speedway supposedly ran in an oval loop just south of I-485 along Industrial Drive, circling to N Polk St./South Blvd.

COST Free

PRO TIP Today, the only hint of the past is a small road named Cadillac Street that runs in what would have been the middle of the track. Its wood was taken and used for lumber during WWII, and nothing remains of the original facility.

of 130 mph. Unfortunately, racing on wooden tracks was just as dangerous as you might imagine, with boards often popping up on the track, and in 1927, just three years after its opening, the speedway closed. It would be 1960 before what we now consider Charlotte Motor Speedway opened to the north of town.

84 ON CALL

Where is Charlotte's most aesthetically appealing cell tower?

Queen's University in historic Myers Park, is one of the area's most picturesque colleges. Founded in 1857, the school moved to its current location in 1914. Red brick pathways lead to traditional brick buildings located around the tree-filled campus.

In the center of campus is a 140-foot tower that is a focus point for those walking between dorms and classrooms. Designed by Jenkins Peer Architects, the tower features asymmetrical windows along its shaft, a clock closer to its base, and a hint of Italian campanile architecture that mixes well with the more historic surrounding buildings. While the clock tower may look traditional, it wasn't constructed until 1997.

Although its exterior is used as an emblem for the University on items like stationary, the tower's interior

---

While its tower isn't necessarily historical, Queens University does have a rich history in Charlotte. Founded in 1857 as the Charlotte Female Institute (it became coeducational after World War II as universities filled with returning veterans), the school became Queens College in 1912 and moved to its current location in 1914.

QUEENS UNIVERSITY OF CHARLOTTE CLOCK TOWER

WHAT The 140-foot tower in the middle of Queens University campus

WHERE 1900 Selwyn Ave.

COST Free

PRO TIP Grab a coffee while you're there from the Coffee House inside the Everett Library. Even though it's a campus hangout, the Coffee House has become a favorite for locals as well for its fireplace and cozy seating area.

Sure, this traditional tower in the center of Queen's University may look like a historical landmark. But it was actually built in 1997 and conceals several cell phone antennae.

actually supports a more practical purpose. The tower conceals three sets of cell phone antennae, carrying signals for national carriers. Its upper design actually includes radio frequency transparent fiberglass so that cell signals can be easily transmitted—all while the tower still looks like a historic bell tower.

85 ALL ABOARD

Why is there a coal-burning steam locomotive permanently parked in Freedom Park?

Since 1959, there's been an unusual find in the middle of Freedom Park. Nestled among the park's picturesque lake and trails, between its sports fields and creek, is an old locomotive that traveled many miles before ending up in its now permanent parking place.

The Gaineseville-Midland 301 was made in Philadelphia in 1920 and shipped to Florida, where it pulled cars between small towns on the state's coast for more than three decades. In 1951, it was purchased by Gainesville-Midland, which gave it the number 301, and for eight years it went back and forth between Gainesville and Athens, GA.

By 1959, steam engines were becoming less popular as diesel engine trains took over the tracks. The city of Charlotte had asked a company called Seaboard for a locomotive to display. That year, Seaboard purchased Gainesville-Midland and its 301, which they deemed the perfect gift for the Queen City.

When the train first arrived in the park, it was advertised as a great spot for kids to play. There was also an old fire truck and a tank at one point—all in place for children to climb and jump on, and enjoy. Today, the fire truck and tank are gone, and when the park was renovated in 1995, play on the train became restricted.

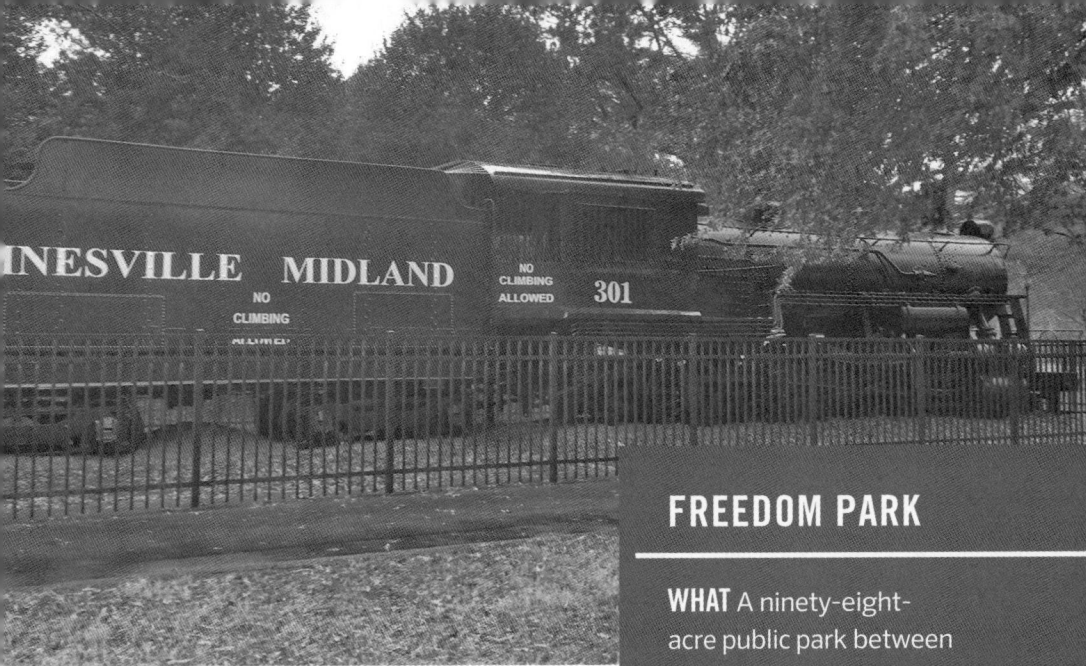

This historic locomotive has been a destination in Freedom Park since 1959, originally serving as a place for children to play. Today, it's fenced off, but still attracts the attention of all ages.

FREEDOM PARK

WHAT A ninety-eight-acre public park between Charlotte's historic Dilworth and Myers Park neighborhoods

WHERE 1900 East Blvd.

COST Free

PRO TIP Today, the train has been repainted with the number and name it had when it originally arrived in Charlotte. You'll find it near the park's central parking lot.

The old locomotive rolled into town that fall and was installed at Freedom Park with a new paint job and a new name: The Freedom Park Express. Originally, it served as glorified playground equipment with children crawling across and under it. But eventually that was seen as dangerous and the train is now in a fenced off area, with access to only its conductor's chamber for those who want to get a taste of transportation during the early part of the twentieth century.

86 ELEPHANT ON THE LOOSE

Why does a grave in Charlotte's Elmwood Cemetery feature an elephant standing beneath a palm tree?

In the 1880s, a group called the John Robinson Circus was traveling around the country and performing for enthusiastic crowds. That September, when the circus came to Charlotte, it brought an elephant named Chief, his mate Mary, and their calf known as The Boy, along with the trainer for all of them, a man named John King.

On September 27, Chief had what some called a fit from a surge of testosterone and crushed John King with his weight, pushing King against his own cage. He then ran up the Trade Street railroad tracks to 5th Street before crossing Tyron. He was finally caught on Church Street.

King died the following day from the injuries, and a hearse pulled by four white horses took him to Charlotte's Elmwood Cemetery. Mary and The Boy walked in their trainer's funeral procession. King was buried beneath an almost five-foot-tall grave that includes an engraving of an elephant standing beneath a palm tree.

The funeral procession for John King is reported to have been elaborate and eye catching. His hearse was pulled by four white horses to Elmwood Cemetery. Circus workers carried the coffin, two other elephants joined the march, and the circus band played at the burial.

JOHN KING GRAVE

WHAT The grave of the elephant trainer who died in Charlotte

WHERE Elmwood Cemetery, 700 W 6th St., section A2

COST Free

PRO TIP Wonder what happened to Chief? After being moved to the Cincinnati Zoo, he killed two more trainers before being put down—and then was served for dinner at Cincinnati's Palace hotel.

This grave at the edge of Uptown's Elmwood Cemetery tells the unusual story of the elephant trainer John King who was tragically killed by an elephant named Chief.

87 THE UPTOWN BUZZ

Why are eighty thousand honeybees living at Uptown's Ritz-Carlton?

Charlotte's Uptown Ritz-Carlton is serious about its commitment to preserving the environment—especially for a hotel smack in the middle of an urban area. It's a LEED Gold-certified hotel with eco-friendly touches like electric vehicle charging stations, a bike valet, and complimentary transportation with hybrid vehicles.

But the hotel's ultimate natural touch is its eighteenth-floor vegetated roof featuring eighteen thousand sedum plants, a chef's garden, and two fully-contained beehives. The hives both assist in pollination for the plants and create honey that the hotel uses in many of its most popular dishes and drinks.

Randall York, who is the owner of Charlotte's popular Cloister Honey, is the beekeeper for the hives. Each year, several gallons of honey are harvested. Want to

---

The honey isn't the only rooftop ingredient you'll find served at Uptown's Ritz-Carlton. Its chic Punch Room bar uses the roof's garden harvest in both its dishes and cocktails. From herbs like mint and basil, to veggies like peppers and cucumbers, many of the items from the verdant garden are plucked for fresh ingredients and garnishes in the swanky fifteenth floor bar.

The Ritz-Carlton's rooftop includes herb and vegetable gardens as well as several beehives. You can enjoy the hotel's rooftop honey in many of its dishes and drinks.

sample the sweet treat? Try the Honey Pecan Gelato or honey macarons served at the hotel's Bar Cocoa, or taste one of the cocktails served at the lobby bar or fifteenth-floor Punch Room. Better yet, luxuriate in one of the honey-based treatments at the hotel's spa.

THE RITZ-CARLTON, UPTOWN CHARLOTTE

WHAT Charlotte's Uptown luxury and LEED Gold-certified hotel

WHERE 201 E Trade St.

COST Rooftop tours are free

PRO TIP On Saturdays at 10 a.m. guests and the public can meet in the hotel's lobby for a Green Behind-the-Scenes tour, which includes the roof garden and beehives. For the ultimate taste of both, visit The Punch Room cocktail bar on the fifteenth floor, where mixologist Bob Peters is known for using the fresh honey and herbs in his creative drinks.

88 FANTASTICAL FIGURINES

Why did Davidson have a museum dedicated to gnomes?

Tom Clark was a Davidson College graduate who returned to the school as a theology professor. In 1985, though, he left the college to devote himself full time to a hobby that had become a thriving business—crafting gnomes. His whimsical figurines, which he sculpted in his studio, gained a worldwide following. So, in the 1980s the famed sculptor purchased the building at 131 N Main St. in Davidson and turned it into a gnome museum and shop, to celebrate and share his beloved gnomes.

The Cairn Studio housed more than one thousand gnomes and was a popular tourist destination until its closing in 2009. Today, Clark, who is now in his late 80s, has stopped producing the gnomes for retail. But his love for Davidson lives on.

As the now-owner of several buildings on its charming Main Street, he has been careful in his choices for the specialty shops and restaurants housed in his buildings. The most notable is Kindred, which has garnered national

---

In addition to his gnomes and woodspirits, Tom Clark is also known for his intricately detailed miniatures of historical figures. He has created hundreds of portrait busts for figures from King David to Beethoven to Davy Crockett.

KINDRED RESTAURANT

WHAT National award-winning restaurant in downtown Davidson

WHERE 131 N Main St., Davidson

COST Prices for food vary, but this is an upscale restaurant

PRO TIP When Joe and Katy Kindred decided they wanted to open their eponymous restaurant on Main Street, they knew they had to convince Clark to rent them the space. The story goes that the two of them arrived at his home with their arms full of food and cooked an excellent meal to convince him. Stop by for dinner and you'll understand why he agreed to have the couple as tenants.

Kindred restaurant, which has garnered national acclaim in recent years, is in the location of what was once Davidson's most unusual attraction—a museum dedicated entirely to gnomes.

attention since its 2015 opening—in the former location of his museum dedicated to gnomes. Now, when locals are enjoying meals in the acclaimed restaurant, they can thank the retired professor and artist for also sculpting their town.

89 FINAL DESTINATION

Where can you step back in time to a 1950s airport?

Charlotte's first airport opened in 1936, not far from the main terminal of its current international airport (its original passenger terminals still stand). Then, in 1954, Charlotte Douglas Municipal Airport opened. At seventy-thousand-square feet, it was the largest airport in the region and with fifty-seven weekday departures by 1957, it was the busiest in the Carolinas.

In 1974, the airport would attract national attention for a tragedy. On the morning of September 11, Eastern Air Lines Flight 212 was scheduled to land in Charlotte, having come from Charleston. The plane crashed during a foggy approach and it was later discovered that the disaster may have been caused by pilot error. Seventy-one people died in the crash, including the father and two older brothers of now-famous comedian Stephen Colbert.

Despite this tragedy, the airport continued to grow and expand. Then, in 1979 ground was broken on a new terminal across the runway, which would become the current

---

In 1941, Charlotte Douglas Municipal Airport was named for Ben Elbert Douglas, Sr., who was the Mayor of Charlotte from 1935 to 1941. Douglas was known for numerous advancements around Charlotte, including being a proponent of the then-controversial construction of Independence Boulevard.

FORMER CHARLOTTE DOUGLAS MUNICIPAL AIRPORT SITE

WHAT The location that was Charlotte's airport from 1954 to 1982

WHERE 4700 Yorkmont Rd.

COST Not open to the public

PRO TIP The building houses private offices, but a drive around the perimeter offers a peek into the past.

For the feeling of stepping back in time, take a drive to the former location of Charlotte's airport, which was built in 1954. Adjacent to the current airport, the former airport site offers a peek of city's traveling history.

main terminal. That same year, Piedmont Airlines chose Charlotte as a hub, and when the new 325,000-square-foot terminal opened in 1982, it was for an airport already gaining notice on the national stage. (Today, it's the 6th busiest airport in the country.)

Fortunately, in a city that often tears down its history, the 1950s municipal airport still stands. Used as an office building, the current space still maintains plenty of traces of its past. Its mid-century modern design can be seen in both its façade and in interior touches like terrazzo tile floors and the free-hanging stairwell. Though its storefronts have long since closed and the wide concourses have since been demolished, the space still offers a glimpse of Charlotte's traveling past.

90 BOMBS AWAY

Why is there something that looks like a missile on a Charlotte street corner?

The Paw Creek neighborhood in the northwestern part of Charlotte was named for a stream that flows through the area toward the Catawba River. It's said that the stream was named by Native Americans for the pawpaw trees that grow along its banks.

It's in this quiet, suburban neighborhood that you'll find one of the city's most unusual sights. At the corner of Paw Creek and Toddville Roads is something that appears at first glance to be a missile.

The structure, which sits in the parking lot between a small business building and the road, was built during the Cuban missile crisis. Arleigh Deyton, who passed away in 2013, was then the owner of Deyton Sheet Metal and built the faux missile to show off his skills with sheet metal. But those in the neighborhood believed he also had a political message behind his work, which features a small American flag and the words "United States" on its side.

Arleigh Deyton built his "missile" during the 1960s. Just a few miles closer to Uptown Charlotte, in 1956, the Charlotte Ordnance Missile Plant (later the Charlotte Army Missile Plant) began crafting real versions, including Nike Ajax missiles and Nike Hercules missiles.

DEYTON'S MISSILE

WHAT A large piece of metal built in the 1960s and made to look like a missile

WHERE The corner of Paw Creek and Toddville Roads

COST Not open to the public

PRO TIP Deyton had some first-hand knowledge of war. The North Carolina native owned Deyton Sheet Metal for more than fifty years, but prior to that he worked for the Navy during World War II in Panama and Hawaii.

Yes, this structure in a predominantly residential neighborhood appears to be a missile. But it's actually a piece of metal built in the 1960s to show off the craftsmanship available at Deyton Sheet Metal, the business formerly at the site.

Either way, the Cold War has ended, and Deyton's fake missile still stands—now an unexpected reminder of a different time in Charlotte and the country's history.

91 PIE IN THE SKY

What's the story behind "The World's Best Pecan Pie" sign on Elizabeth Avenue?

After sixty years in business, Andersons Restaurant shut its doors in 2006. And while it had been a casual restaurant, known for its simple breakfasts and sweet pecan pie, Andersons was much more than just a dining destination.

Jimmie Anderson originally opened the restaurant in 1946 as Mercury Sandwich Shop. Over the years, the family-run spot with its Formica tables and red booths became a favorite for the powerful and political set. Former Bank of America CEO Hugh McColl regularly stopped in for coffee, while former Senator Elizabeth Dole and Mayor Richard Vinroot were often found chatting with other diners over pancake breakfasts.

But this was also the kind of place with neighborhood regulars. Its close proximity to the nearby hospital meant that staff there often stopped in for a quick coffee before work or breakfast after an overnight shift. Andersons was a beloved landmark.

In addition to its famed pecan pie and chocolate pecan pie, Andersons now offers a catering menu for delivery as well. Its comfort food choices like pancakes or biscuits for breakfast and chicken and dumplings or meat loaf at lunch will feel familiar to former patrons of the famed brick and mortar spot.

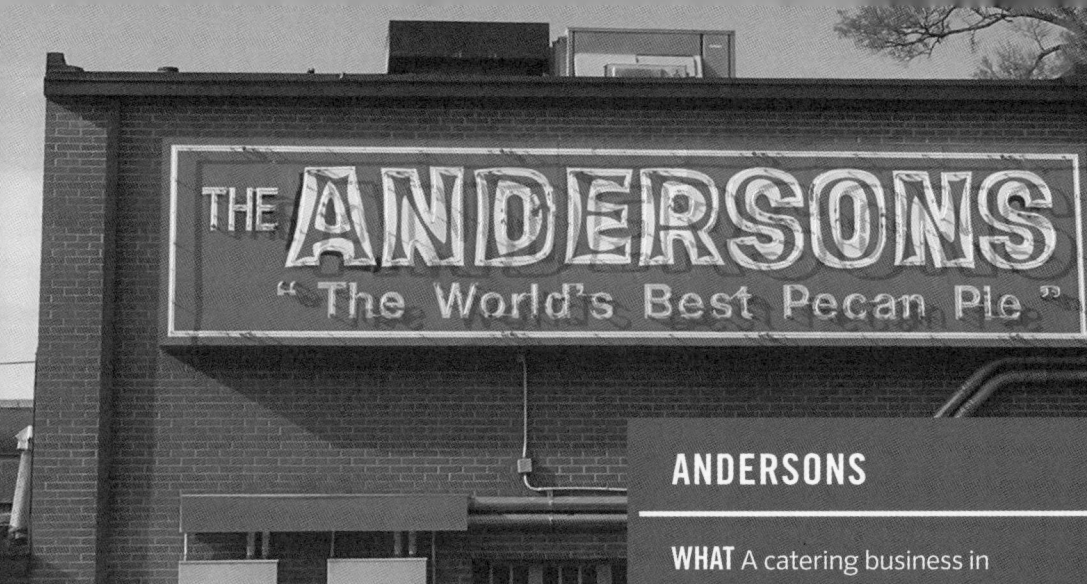

Andersons Restaurant may have closed in 2006, but the business continues to offer its famed pies by order at its small location behind Viva Kitchen on Elizabeth Avenue.

And so, when it shut its doors and began running a catering and pie delivery service, Andersons moved its sign and its self-proclaimed "World's Best" pecan pie to the back of the original building, where you can still see it today.

ANDERSONS

WHAT A catering business in Elizabeth with a vintage sign advertising its famed pie

WHERE 1617 Elizabeth Ave. (behind Viva Chicken)

COST The "World's Best" pecan pie is $24

PRO TIP You can order Andersons pies via the company's website (www.andersonsdelivery.com) and you can see the sign best from Hawthorne Lane. The former restaurant location was turned first into a Starbucks and is now a Viva Chicken, bearing no real resemblance to its notable predecessor.

92 HOME SWEET HOME

What are the two small houses on the grounds behind Old Little Rock A.M.E. Zion Church in Uptown?

Driving down 7th Street on your way out of Uptown you'll see skyscrapers, the light rail, a new market, and... two tiny "shotgun" houses from the early twentieth century. The two small, white houses tucked in the lot behind Little Rock A.M.E. Zion Church are basically all that's left of a time when these homes filled the streets of Uptown.

Generally found in African American neighborhoods, rows of these homes were once squeezed into places like First and Third Wards, as well as Brooklyn and Villa Heights. The simple houses, which you'll find around the country, are especially popular in New Orleans and said to have originated in Haiti. Commonly, it's thought that the term "shotgun home" came from the idea that you could open the front and back doors and shoot a gun through without hitting any walls. But as that's not true in many models, it seems likely the term

---

These two shotgun homes were originally built at 153 and 155 West Bland Street. The neighborhood, now known as South End, was called Blandville and filled with similar homes. The "urban renewal" program of the 1960s and 1970s pushed out the neighborhood's homes in favor of industrial buildings. Now, the neighborhood is shifting once again as townhomes stand where these houses once were.

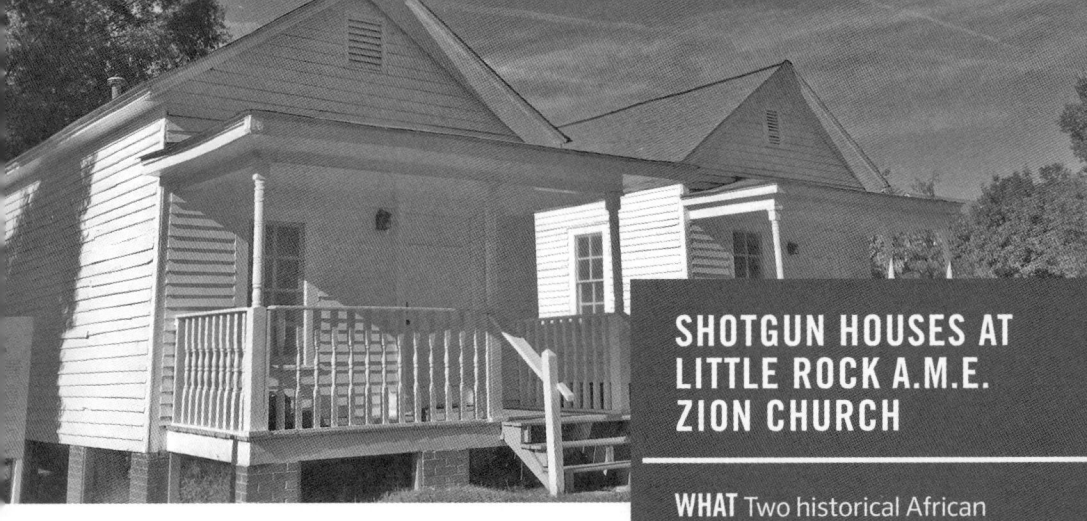

While almost all of Uptown's original shotgun homes were destroyed in the 1960s and 1970s, these two houses behind Little Rock A.M.E. Zion Church remain as reminders of the city's past.

SHOTGUN HOUSES AT LITTLE ROCK A.M.E. ZION CHURCH

WHAT Two historical African American homes, likely built in the late 1890s and moved to the current location in 1986

WHERE 403 N Myers St.

COST Not currently open to the public

PRO TIP For a close-up look at the homes, turn into the church's parking lot. From the exterior you can see features like the brick chimneys, front porches, and paned windows.

doesn't have anything to do with a gun and is actually a version of a Haitian word first used to describe them.

In Charlotte, in the 1960s and 1970s, the city destroyed most of these homes as part of its so-called urban renewal program. Then, in 1986, Little Rock A.M.E. became Charlotte's Afro-American Cultural Center, and the two homes there now were moved from their original location on Bland Street with the idea of making them part of the center's exhibits.

Today, the church has purchased back the property, but the two homes remain owned by the cultural center, which is now located on South Tryon Street in the Harvey B. Gantt Center. There have been various proposals for ways to once again bring these historically significant homes into the city's spotlight. But for now, the two quietly sit adjacent to the parking lot behind the church, occasionally catching the eye of passersby.

93 A GRAVE AFFAIR

Why is there a cemetery within a cemetery in Uptown Charlotte?

As you walk around Uptown's large Elmwood cemetery, you'll notice something strange. In the back corner there seems to be an area that is separated from the rest of the graveyard. It's a large field with scattered headstones and its own pathways. A sign marks its entrance from the main cemetery: 9th Street Pinewood Cemetery, Established 1853.

Elmwood was also established in 1853 and its first burial took place in 1855, but it was a cemetery only for white people. Following the Civil War, many of its plots were purchased and burials included large and intricate tombstones and mausoleums. Pinewood, which was adjacent to it, was for African Americans. There, the tombstones were less detailed or only small markers in the ground—and often there are no remaining markers at all.

African Americans were only allowed to enter the graveyard from the 9th Street entrance and a fence was even installed

---

Taking down the fence between Elmwood and Pinewood cemeteries was no small feat. During the civil rights movement, a group of African American leaders in Charlotte, led by the city's first black city councilman, Fred Alexander, argued for its removal. In January of 1969, the then-mayor, Stan R. Brookshire, broke a tie in the city council with his vote to finally remove it.

Uptown's Elmwood cemetery includes a section called Pinewood Cemetery, which was once for African Americans. The fence that separated the two graveyards wasn't taken down until 1969.

ELMWOOD AND PINEWOOD CEMETERY

WHAT The historical cemetery located in Uptown Charlotte

WHERE Take 6th St. west leading out of Uptown. One block past the Graham St. intersection, the entrance to Elmwood is on your right.

COST Free

PRO TIP Look for the grave of George Miller, a man who was born a slave and died free around the age of 75 in 1925. According to the headstone, he was "All of his life, a loyal and faithful servant of R. M. Miller, Sr." The headstone was erected by R.M. Miller, Jr.

between the two cemeteries. Eventually, it became illegal to discriminate in burial plots, but the fence wouldn't be taken down until 1969. Today, two roads run parallel to each other where the fence once stood between them—a striking reminder of the city's divided past. But the cemetery is now one large burial ground, accessible to everyone from all sides.

94 SOMETHING'S FISHY

Does a monster lurk beneath the waters of Lake Norman?

Lake Norman is a man-made lake, completed in 1964, so it shouldn't be a mystery what's beneath its surface. After all, there are many people still living who remember the land prior to its being covered with water. But that doesn't keep locals from speculating on lore about a monster that is said to have been spotted in its depths.

There are many different versions of "Normie," as it's called by those around the lake. In some, the monster has a fin and large sharp teeth while in others, it's a giant creature, so large it can knock over boats. It's been spotted all around the lake, but most sightings seem to occur near the Cowan's Ford dam.

Assuming it's not an actual monster, there are a few theories as to what boaters and swimmers may be

---

The children's book isn't the only published work on "Normie." Since 2002, a website called LakeNormanMoster.com has asked those who have seen the monster to share their experiences. In 2012, author Matthew Myers collected those sightings and turned them into a book called *Lake Norman Monster: A Decade of Sightings*.

For an unusual twist on your next Lake Norman boating experience, taking a fishing trip with Captain Gus and ask about the lake's supposed monster, "Normie."

LAKE CRUISE WITH CAPT. GUS

WHAT Take a trip on the lake with acclaimed fishing guide Capt. Gus Gustafson.

WHERE Book at a trip on Lake Norman at www.fishingwithgus.com

COST Prices vary

PRO TIP Capt. Gus has lived in the area since 1960 and knows the lake well. He has his own ideas about the creature, and he's guided cruises on the lake for those interested in searching for Normie.

seeing in the lake's waters. Some say that catfish near the dam have grown to five or six feet long. Others suggest that large carp, fresh water eels, and snakeheads may be what people have seen.

Regardless of Normie's origins, the tale is so popular it has spawned a local children's book, *Normie the Lake Norman Monster*. He may not be real, but locals love to talk about the famed fish creature.

95. THE BIG CHEESE

How did Charlotte earn the title of pimento cheese capital of the world?

In recent years, pimento cheese, the tasty mixture of shredded cheese, mayonnaise, and peppers, has become a go-to comfort food in homes around the country. But the dish actually has its origins in the working class South. Georgia has long been a large producer of pimentos and some say the mixture was originally created because the peppers would keep flies away from the cheese.

Regardless of how the recipe came to be, by the early part of the twentieth century, pimento cheese was being used on sandwiches as a cheap and easy lunch, especially for those working in textile mills. The cheese made for a cheaper source of protein during the Depression, and in 1953, a small kitchen on Wilkinson Boulevard began producing tubs of it to sell to local grocers. Ruth's Salads, owned by Bob Miller, quickly expanded and began selling its cheese to chain supermarkets, requiring a move into a larger facility.

Today, Ruth's is still based in Charlotte, and family owned and operated—and is the top pimento cheese producer in the

---

Ruth's Salads was selling its beloved pimento cheese in area grocery stores that are now part of history themselves. Food Town (now known as Food Lion) and Harris Supermarkets (now known as Harris-Teeter) were two of the first spots where locals could find the creamy dish.

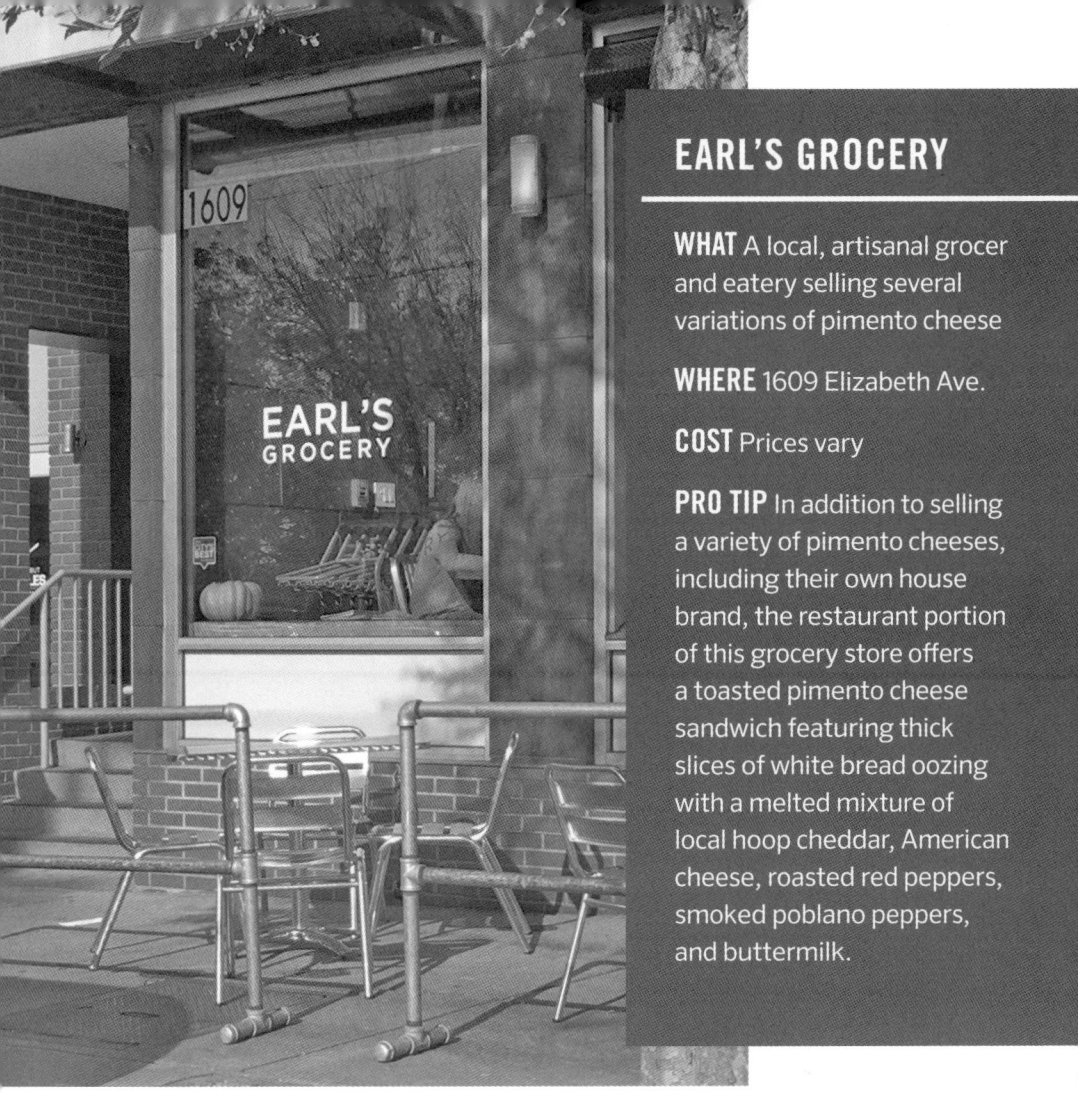

EARL'S GROCERY

WHAT A local, artisanal grocer and eatery selling several variations of pimento cheese

WHERE 1609 Elizabeth Ave.

COST Prices vary

PRO TIP In addition to selling a variety of pimento cheeses, including their own house brand, the restaurant portion of this grocery store offers a toasted pimento cheese sandwich featuring thick slices of white bread oozing with a melted mixture of local hoop cheddar, American cheese, roasted red peppers, smoked poblano peppers, and buttermilk.

While there are countless restaurants, grocery stores, and shops around town to get your pimento cheese fix, Earl's Grocery in Elizabeth features a creamy housemade version worth a taste.

country. They produce around forty-five thousand pounds per week of the spread. And they're in the right place for it. North Carolina is also the largest consumer of the dish in the country, with Charlotte ranking at the top of the state for indulging in the cheesy mix.

INDEX

5Church, 170-171
7th Street Market, 12-13
African American, 49, 176, 202, 203, 204, 205
Alaska Heritage Museum, 162
Alexander, Fred, 204
Alexander Michael's, 51
Ambrose, 2-3
Amelie's French Bakery, 72-73, 91
American Asset Corporation, 8
American Legion Memorial Stadium, 24
Amity Presbyterian Church, 60, 61
Anderson, Jimmie, 200
Andersons Restaurant, 200-201
Appalachian Mountains, 18, 111
Arco, Count Riprand, 8
Arlington Building, 142-143
Art of War, The, 170, 171
Asheville, 6, 28
Asian Herald, The, 108
Asian Library, 94, 108-109
Astor, The, 150-151
Atherton Mill and Market, 46-47, 138
Atlanta, 10, 62, 170, 171
Auten, Greg, 36
Avant Fuel & Ice Company, 38
Avett Brothers, The, 44
Bakker, Jim, 30
Bakker, Tammy Faye, 30
Ballentine, Jim, 116
Bank of America, 6-7, 13, 18, 64-65, 78, 90, 128, 129, 141, 200
Bates, Lewis F., 76
Battle of the Bulge, 74
BB&T Ballpark, 14-15
Bechtler, Andreas, 62
Bechtler Museum of Modern Art, 42, 57, 62-63, 78
Beethoven, Ludwig von, 194
Belhaven University, 156
Belmont, 160-161
Belmont Abbey College, 160-161
Bernadin's, 74-75
Bible, The, 60, 82, 83

Billy Graham Library, 66-67, 107
Blum, Nancy, 129
Bojangles Coliseum, 130-131
Booty Loop, 133, 145
Boston Red Sox, 17
Bottomley, William L., 68
Brewer, J.P., 178
Brooklyn, 202
Brookshire, Stan R., 204
Burgushi, 10, 11
Calvert, Bill, 121
Camp Greene, 88-89
Campbell, Paul, 17
cankerworms, 144, 145
Cannon, Frances, 112
Cardenas, Lazaro, 83
Cardenas Museum, 82, 83
Carillon Building, 42-43
Carolina Panthers, 128, 147
Carolina Raptor Center, 114-115
Carolina Voices, 157
Carolinas Aviation Museum, 4-5
Catawba River, 52, 88, 180, 181, 198
CBS, 42
cemeteries, 2, 3, 16, 17, 60, 190, 191, 204, 205
Cerny, David, 8, 9
Charles, Ray, 131
Charleston, 170, 171, 196
Charlotte Bobcats, 25
Charlotte Checkers, 131
Charlotte Douglas International Airport, 4, 5, 23, 48, 122, 123, 196
Charlotte Douglas Municipal Airport, 196-197
Charlotte Hornets, 24-25, 128
Charlotte Knights, 14-15, 24
Charlotte Liberty Walk, 40, 120
Charlotte Motor Speedway, 18-19, 184-185
Charlotte News, The, 89, 153
Charlotte Observer, 2, 29, 46, 128, 152
Charlotte Transportation Center, 128-129
Chevrolet, 82
Chicago White Sox, 14
Christ, Jesus, 31, 126-127
Christmas, 34, 66, 156, 157, 178
Chun, Ki-Hyun, 108

Civil War, 2, 20, 26, 76, 110, 158, 204
Clark, Tom, 194-195
Clinton, Chelsea, 55
Cloister Honey, 192
Coca-Cola, 18
Colbert, Stephen, 196
Comida, 116-117
Cone, Bonnie, 148, 149
Confederacy, 26, 76, 77
Cook's Inn, 164-165
Copperfield, David, 42, 43
Cornwallis, General, 24, 25
Cowfish Sushi Burger Bar, 10-11
Crockett, Davy, 194
Daimler, 69
Dairy Queen, 22-23
Dali, Salvador, 135
Danes, Claire, 174
Davidson, 126, 127, 194, 195
Davidson College, 194
Davis, Jefferson, 76, 77
de Saint Phalle, Niki, 42, 56, 62, 63, 78
Declaration of Independence, 78, 120, 121
Deyton, Arleigh, 198, 199
DH Griffin Wrecking Company, 42
Diamant, Jeff, 29
Dilworth, 46, 84, 138, 144, 175, 189
Discovery Place, 124-125
Disney World, 30
Disneyland, 30
Dog Bar, The, 178-179
Dole, Elizabeth, 200
Douglas, Ben Elbert, Sr., 196
Dowd Family, 89
Dowd House, 92-93
Duke Energy, 52-53, 112
Duke Energy Center, 146-147
Duke, James B., 112
Duke Mansion, 95, 112-113, 174
Duke University, 112
Dunhill Hotel, 70-71
Dylan, Bob, 131
Earl's Grocery, 209
Eastland Mall, 152

Eastover, 27, 142
Ed's Tavern, 175
Elizabeth, 138, 139, 182-183, 201, 209
Elmwood Cemetery, 190, 191, 204-205
Emory University, 135
Fagan, Chas, 121
Fat Parrot, 174
Federal Aviation Administration, 52
Federal Bureau of Investigation, 29
Federal Reserve Bank, 48
Firebird, 42, 62-63, 78
First Presbyterian Church, 2, 3
Food Network, 36
Ford, Henry, 58
Ford Motor Company, 58, 59, 138
Forest Lawn West Cemetery, 16, 17
Fox, 174
Freedom Park, 106, 188-189
Frew, Archibald, 34
Galifianakis, Zach, 28, 29
Gantt, Harvey B., 203
Georgia, 76, 208
Ghantt, David Scott, 28, 29
ghosts, 2, 12, 34, 35, 71
gold, 1, 20, 21, 26, 27, 48, 64, 65, 148, 158
Gold Line Streetcar, 139, 182
Gold Rush Trolley, 20, 64
Gourmajenko, Alexis, 68
Graham, Billy, 60, 66, 80, 130, 131
Graham, Ruth Bell, 67
Great Depression, 58, 70, 85, 208
Green, Robert, 80
Green, The, 56-57, 75
Green's Lunch, 80-81
Greenspan, Alan, 48
Greenville, 164
Gross, Jim, 142
Grotto of Our Lady of Lourdes, 160-161
Gustafson, Gus, 207
Hall, Marcus, 10
Hampton, Henry, 166
Harvard University, 112
Heisenberg, Werner, 177
Heist Brewery, 136-137

Helmick, Ralph, 176-177
Helms, Jesse, 54-55
Heritage USA, 1, 30-31
Hersey, John, 112
Hilton, Daisy, 16-17
Hilton, Violet, 16-17
Home Run Dragon, 14
Homeland, 113, 174, 175
Homeless Jesus, 126-127
Homer the Dragon, 15
Hong Kong Flu, 17
Hope, Bob, 16
Hornets Fan Shop, 24
Hotel Charlotte, 42-43
Howell, Mills, 170
Hudson River, 4, 5
Hunger Games, The, 174
Hurricane Hugo, 30
Il Grande Disco, 78
Independence Square, 49
Internal Revenue Service, 30
Iredell Museums, 135
Jack, James, 120, 121
Jackson, Andrew, 82
Janney, Christopher, 12
Jefferson, Thomas, 120
Johnson, Junior, 154-155
Joliet, 22
Kahn, Albert, 59
Kaskey, Ramond, 48, 122
Kennedy, Jacqueline, 131
Kennedy, John F., 112
Keys, Alicia, 131
King David, 194
King, John, 190, 191
Kindred, Joe, 195
Kindred, Katy, 195
Kindred Restaurant, 194-195
Knight Theater, 156-157, 174
Kolwitz, Kathe, 135
La Guardia Airport, 4
Lake Norman, 1, 52, 53, 99, 206, 207
Lakewood Park, 84
Last Supper, 31

Latta, Edward Dilworth, 84
Lazy 5 Ranch, 166-167
Legend, John, 131
Leno, Jay, 168, 169
Letterman, David, 131
Levine Cancer Institute, 133
Lewis, Damian, 174
Lincoln, Abraham, 76, 77
Little Rock A.M.E. Zion Church, 202-203
Little Sugar Creek Greenway, 152-153
livermush, 1, 80, 110, 111
Long, Benjamin, 6
Loomis, Fargo & Co., 28, 29
Margaret the Mummy, 134-135
Marshall Park, 174
Masterminds, 29
McColl, Hugh, 128, 129, 141, 200
McCormick & Schmick's, 77
McGill, Helen, 38
McGill, Henry, 38
McGill Rose Garden, 38-39
McGuire, Jim, 172
McManaway, Hugh, 140, 141
McNinch, S.S., 51
Meck Dec Day, 120-121
Metalmorphosis, 8-9
Metropolitan Shopping Center, 108, 152, 153
Midtown, 94, 108, 152, 153
Miller, Bob, 208
Miller, George, 205
Miller, R.M, Jr. 205
Miller, R.M, Sr., 205
Mint Museum, 1, 26-27, 57
Monroe, 32, 33, 54
moonshine, 18, 154
MorningStar Fellowship Church, 30, 31
Morrison, Cameron, 60
Museum of the Alphabet, 82-83
Myers, Matthew, 206
Myers Park, 68, 95, 96-97, 112, 132, 133, 138, 140, 142, 144, 145, 174, 186, 189
NASA, 59
NASCAR Hall of Fame, 18, 118, 119, 154-155, 185
National Basketball Association, 24, 25, 168

National Football League, 80, 168
NationsBank, 128, 129
Native American, 40, 180, 181, 198
Neighborhood Theatre, 102-103, 150-151
New Orleans Hornets, 25
New Orleans Pelicans, 25
New York, 4, 24, 68
Newton, Cam, 80
Nikko Japanese Restaurant and Sushi Bar, 143
Nix, Joanna, 143
Nixon, Richard, 131
NoDa, 72, 102-103, 136, 137, 150, 151, 178, 179
Noland, Kenneth, 135
Nordan, Dianne, 32
Nordan, Phil, 32
Norm the Niner, 148-149
Normie, the Lake Norman Monster, 206-207
Norris, Jon, 170
North Carolina, 4, 22, 26, 28, 32, 49, 54, 64, 108, 110, 121, 129, 134, 135, 136, 137, 148, 149, 160, 162, 163, 199, 209
North Carolina, University of, 114, 122, 123, 148, 149, 159
Odell, A.G., 86
Old Settlers' Cemetery, 2-3
Open Kitchen, 36
Overstreet Mall, 86-87
Paw Creek, 198, 199
Pearl Harbor, 58
Penguin Drive-In, 36, 116, 117
Pennsylvania, 111, 134, 184
Persistence of Vision, 176-177
Peters, Bob, 193
Philadelphia, 120, 121, 134, 158, 188
Pinewood Cemetery, 204-205
Pinky's Westside Grill, 1, 36-37
Plaza Midwood, 116, 117, 172, 173
Poe, Edgar Allan, 56
Polk, James K., 3
Polk, Thomas, 3, 164, 165
Pomodoro, Arnaldo, 78
Pope Francis, 127
Presbyterian Hospital, 139
Presley, Elvis, 29, 42, 131
Price's Chicken Coop, 168-169
Prohibition, 18, 44

PTL Club, 30
Puckett's Farm Equipment, 44-45
Queen Charlotte, 48, 122-123, 132
Queen's Table, 122-123
Queen's University, 141, 186-187
Raleigh, 10
Ramsey Creek Park, 53
Ratcliffe, Louis G., 74
Ratcliffe, Louis, Jr., 74
Red Cross, 26
Reed, Conrad, 20
Reed Gold Mine, 20-21, 148
Reed, John, 20
Revolutionary War, 52, 180
Reynolds, Blanche, 68, 69
Ritz-Carlton, 100-101, 175, 192-193
Rolling Stones, The, 131
Romare Bearden Park, 15
Roosevelt, Franklin D., 42
Rosedale Plantation, 34-35
RuRu's Taco & Tequila, 69
Saint Alban's Episcopal Church, 126, 127
Saint Mary's College, 160
Saint Peter's Catholic Church, 6, 56
Saint Vincent Abbey, 160
Santa Claus, 156, 157
Schechter, Stuart, 176
Schmalz, Timothy, 126
Seine River, 72
Seoul, 108
Sharon Presbyterian Church, 60-61
Shaw, Elsie, 141
Shelby, 110, 111
Shelby Café, 111
Showtime, 174, 175
Shuffletown Dragway, 118-119
Simmons, Floyd "Chunk," 17
Sleepy Hollow, 174
South Carolina, 64, 76
South End, 138, 142, 143, 147, 168, 169, 202
South End Mill, 46
SouthPark Mall, 10, 152
Spectrum Center, 24-25, 139
Speedway Club Restaurant, 18

Springsteen, Bruce, 131
Stagioni, 69
Statesville, 135
Sullenberger, Chesley "Sully," 4, 5
TEN Park Lanes, 154
Tinguely, Jean, 42, 43
Tompkins, Daniel Augustus, 46
Torah, The, 82
Touch My Building, 12
Townsend, William Cameron, 82, 83
Trail of Tears, 82
Treehouse Vineyards, 33
Treloar, Julie, 158
Treloar, William, 158, 159
Trolley Walk, 98, 182-183
trolleys, 20, 47, 64, 84, 85, 132, 133, 138, 139, 182, 183
Tuck Fest, 181
Tuckaseegee Trail and Ford, 180, 181
Tzu, Sun, 170
Uptown, 1, 2, 3, 6, 7, 12, 13, 14, 15, 17, 23, 24, 25, 26, 27, 28, 29, 34, 38, 40-41, 42, 48, 50, 51, 56, 57, 58, 59, 62, 63, 64, 66, 70, 71, 74, 75, 77, 78, 80, 81, 86, 87, 120, 124, 125, 129, 138, 139, 142, 143, 47, 150, 154, 155, 157, 158, 162, 164, 165, 170, 171, 173, 174, 176, 177, 182, 185, 191, 192, 198, 202, 203, 204, 205
U.S. National Whitewater Center, 180-181
Villa Heights, 202
Vinroot, Richard, 128, 129, 200
Virgin Mary, The, 160, 161
Volkswagen, 1, 36, 37
Wachovia, 162
Washington DC, 54, 55
Washington, George, 164, 165
Waxhaw, 82, 83
Wells Fargo, 56, 87, 146, 162
Wells Fargo History Museum, 163
Whitehall Corporate Center, 9
Wingate, 54, 55
World War I, 26, 88, 89
World War II, 59, 138, 148, 185, 186, 199
Yadkin Valley, 32
York, Randall, 192